Gardening Letters
to my Daughter

Anne Scott-James

Gardening Letters to my Daughter

WITH SOME REPLIES FROM
Clare Hastings

ILLUSTRATIONS BY
Virginia Powell

St. Martin's Press
New York

Library of Congress Cataloging-in-Publication Data

Scott-James, Anne.
    Gardening letters to my daughter / Anne Scott-James ;
    illustrations by Virginia Powell.
        p.   cm.
    ISBN 0-312-05867-5
    1. Gardening.   2. Scott-James, Anne, 1913- —Correspondence.
    3. Hastings, Clare—Correspondence.   4. Horticultural writers—
    England—Correspondence.   I. Title.
    SB455.S37   1991
    635—dc20   90-26757
                                                                     CIP

First published in Great Britain by Michael Joseph Limited,
The Penguin Group.

First U.S. Edition: May 1991
10 9 8 7 6 5 4 3 2 1

Contents

Introduction

My daughter Clare and I live next door to one another in a small village on the Berkshire downs. My cottage is late eighteenth century, of brick painted white with a tiled roof. Clare's is older and thatched. Both are in the heart of the country with small front gardens and larger gardens at the back, surrounded by hedgerow trees with fields beyond. The ground slopes steeply and lends itself to informal or cottagey gardening, but the views of the downs are so beautiful that one does not regret the lack of planned vistas inside the boundaries. A tall, thick evergreen hedge separates our gardens, with an arch cut out of the middle for easy travel between the two.

I have had my cottage since 1938 and my children were brought up there, at least at weekends and during school holidays. At some time in the 1970s my late husband, Osbert Lancaster, Clare's stepfather, bought the cottage next door, called Bankside, and gave it to Clare so that she could have a country home of her own. It meant we could see each other frequently without getting in each other's hair, and it has been a joy to us both.

Clare did not take to gardening as early in life as I did (I started at about the age of ten), and had owned her cottage for several years before she became impassioned about plants. Now she is an addict, and we talk gardening with equal enthusiasm. Sometimes her daughter, Calypso, joins in and asks for a new alpine plant for her rockery, which is all of four feet by three.

In January last year I felt that I might not be able to manage my own garden much longer, for it is too large for me now that I have reached the creaky years, and I thought it would be fun to record some of my experiences in a series of letters to Clare, hoping she would find them useful or entertaining. I wrote them week by week, sometimes sitting at my garden table with my plants all round me, sometimes at my desk in London. Some of my letters prompted Clare to reply, and I have included her letters among my own.

When I decide that it is time to leave my cottage, I shall not weep for the garden, for next door there is another, younger garden coming along.

Rose Cottage, Spring 1990.

January

Passing the Torch

Dearest Clare,

It is exactly fifty years since I began to make the garden at Rose Cottage, and since you are now making a garden yourself I thought my reflections on the subject might entertain you. So from time to time this year I will write you a letter.

Please stop the correspondence at once if I fall into pomposity. If you catch me uttering aphorisms such as 'soft, subtle colours are more satisfying than bright contrasts', or 'send your roses scrambling up apple trees with clematis in hot pursuit', let me know by return. I know you love my garden, but you are a good gardener yourself in a wild, erratic way, and do many things better than I do, so I want to discuss, not lecture. As the weeks go by, I want to write about plants, design, wild flowers, books, people, successes, failures, just as they occur to me and I would appreciate criticism or questions from you so that there is a two-way traffic. I hope you like this idea.

Your loving Mother.

Dear Mother,

I thought I saw you peering with a certain glint through the gap in the leylandii, eyeing up my random patches of earth.

I should like lots of advice (or, better still, a gardener complete with wellies, a spade and an eye on the cloud formations). As you know, my memory is limited, so please write *everything* down. I forget nearly instantly the name of every flower – and I do prefer a nice English title to a Latin one – but 'I know what I like'. I should like a Beatrix Potter garden. Parsley among the hollyhocks, honeysuckle twisted round the roses, and preferably no effort at all. I assume the last is wishful thinking?

I seem to be extraordinarily bad on scale. I have not got used to the fact that the tiny little shrub will grow into a huge tree, and I have not learnt to put the bedding plants into size order. Also, as my garden is on steep banks, which I find is like landscaping Mount Eiger, I should like a lot of advice on plants for the bone-dry summit; I can cope with the easier valleys at the bottom.

I *am* glad that your garden has taken fifty years, I hadn't realised that you had been ensconced so long. I see that I need not hurry. As you know, I warm to the idea of bulk buying from the garden centre in the morning, planting in the afternoon, and sitting with my Pimms (mint plucked from a brimming herb bed) inhaling flowers by the evening, but I am prepared to embark on a programme of re-education.

Love,
Clare.

Know Your Garden

Dearest Clare,

I wonder if you really know your garden? You will say, 'Of course, I do', as you work every inch of it yourself, with a bit of mowing help from idle weekend guests suffering from guilt. You know that there is nearly half an acre of it and that it surrounds your thatched cottage, which is built on a steep slope of the Berkshire downs. You know that old ramshackle hedges enclose it, and that the garden is mostly grass, with an orchard of plum, greengage and apple trees in the front. You have old roses on the cottage, honeysuckle on the porch and, your pride and joy, a young wisteria on the south wall. You have a wide, wavy border at the foot of the front wall of the cottage planted with alchemilla, nepeta, and other sturdy herbaceous plants; also a few shrubs and bulbs.

The back garden, which is too large for convenience, is again mostly grass, with a dining-table and barbecue in the middle. This back garden is very haphazard, with random clumps of shrubs old and new, including lilac, viburnum and philadelphus, and a bit of copse at the far end. The prettiest bed (of wavy outline – you are right, straight lines do not suit the terrain) slopes down from the far hedge, is sheltered and gets lots of sun: here are primroses in spring, and rugosa roses, small shrubs, hardy geraniums and other ground-cover plants in summer. It is all rather wild and quirky, not to say eccentric, but extremely attractive, and if you consciously designed it you would spoil it.

But your technical knowledge of the garden is skimpy, and in this respect, so often have I visited it in my inquisitive way, I know it better than you do. Which way does it face? What is the soil? What are the local hazards? You ought to know these things if you are not to suffer unnecessary disappointments. In fact, the cottage faces slightly north of west, the soil is highly alkaline, and the garden is very dry and drains too fast, especially at the top of the slope, the soil

being a little moister and heavier at the bottom. The worst
dangers are drought in summer and the south-west wind
which rushes up the valley knocking young plants about
before they are strongly established.

I find it a lovely garden, very true to your character,
impulsively planted but so lovingly cared for that the wildest
gambles come off. And it is growing prettier all the time.

P.S. Thank you for your letter and I will think about scale
and shrubs for dry places. I will battle with you later about
Latin versus English names.

Dear M,

I know my garden best on Sundays. This is when I have
spent the whole weekend up to my armpits in weeds and
general gardening paraphernalia. When I leave off, wrinkled
and worn, there is not an unresearched area. I like late
afternoon on Sunday. It is the one time in the whole
weekend when I feel totally at peace. Lunch has been
disposed of, all the tools put away, and the last visitor has
tootled off, yet this is the moment when I daren't walk round
the garden. Everything to the eye, from a suitable distance,
looks neat and tidy and I pretend that all is under control. I
mustn't amble round admiring my efforts, or before I know it
I'll be back on hands and knees clutching a trowel –
gardening could be added to the dangerous drug list as far as
I'm concerned.

When I return to the country on Friday, the first thing to
greet the eye is grass. Mountains of it. How does it grow so
fast? It should be static in mid-winter but is already sprouting
ominously. This is the most oppressive local hazard.

As you generously point out, my real technical knowledge
is skimpy, in fact I would say non-existent. I know there was
a brick shed built somewhere in the back of my garden at
some point, and the owner was an avid collector of small
glass medicine bottles. I mention this because I am too busy

removing pieces of red brick and segments of glass to notice the soil, although I have spotted the chalk.

I shall have to develop into an instinctive gardener, renowned in the area for my green fingers rather than my scientific know-how. Or, I could ask *you* every time I need to know which way I am facing, and in turn you could ask me how to tune in your car radio. Can we do a deal?

Wild Flowers

Dear Clare,

I have been thinking about the picking of wild flowers, a subject very dear to me as the lonely holidays I spent with John as a child were made radiant by the wild flowers in the woods and fields of Berkshire. As you know, your Uncle John was much handicapped and could not lead a normal life, and it was my task (and pleasure) to look

after him in the holidays, both of us staying as lodgers in a cottage. The cottage was semi-detached and rather ugly, but at the far end of the garden was a brook with a plank across it leading into a magical wood with many oak trees and woodland flowers.

I had at that time a collecting tin and a flower press, and every day we set out with a packet of cream sandwich biscuits and walked as far as we could in search of flowers; these I would press in the evenings when John had gone to bed. Sometimes I left John in the charge of our landlady – a fierce old lady with a moustache who had years before been nanny to a grand family – and went out alone on my bicycle, and I think that few species within a five- or six-mile radius of the cottage can have escaped me. At that time there were many orchids in the woods, cowslips in the fields, and balsam, loosestrife and flowering rushes by the river. My flower book was the Rev C.A. Johns' *Flowers of the Field*, and until later life I knew no other. At this stage I learned only the English names.

Today, flower picking is frowned upon, in many cases forbidden by law, and it has to be so since wild flowers are tragically scarce, but I think that children, especially girls, are missing one of the great experiences of childhood. To pick a flower is so much more satisfying than just observing it, or photographing it, when the mechanics form a barrier between you and the plant. I wish I could draw or paint: that would be a solution.

So in later years I have grown in my garden as many flowers as possible for children to pick. I was not wholly pleased when Calypso, having asked if she could pick a bunch for your kitchen table, worked through my patch of oxlips, but it was my fault for not warning her. Usually she can have loads of snowdrops, aconites, bluebells, lungwort, primroses or Solomon's seal in spring. Summer is more difficult, but even then there are wild geraniums of various sorts, foxgloves, marguerites and scabious.

I throw this out as a thought for your own garden as, like me, you are not too tidy-minded and would like flowers to seed about the place. January is a good time to put in some plants for naturalising, and you could transplant some of my aconites now, and dig up some of my emerging primrose plants and transfer them to your bank. Though supposed to be woodland plants they seed amazingly in my dry, chalky soil.

Winter Flowers

Dear child,

I have been looking out of the window at the winter-flowering cherry, *Prunus subhirtella autumnalis*, which has been in bloom since before Christmas. This tree was a disappointment for its first four years since it insisted on flowering in spring when its delicate cloud of flowers was eclipsed by the apple blossom and the double gean. Then two years ago it got the message and flowered throughout the winter and has now grown into the right habit.

I think the important thing about winter-flowering plants is to grow them near the house. My habitat is the kitchen and I like to see flowers through the window. The best place, horticulturally speaking, for my hellebores is the copsy bit at the far end of the garden where the soil is relatively rich, but to see them means putting on wellies and making an expedition in possibly daunting weather. So I have a few hellebores, including a lovely pure white *H. orientalis*, within eyeshot of the sink, although the soil is a bit dry to be ideal; also within sight is a clump of the earliest dwarf iris in my garden, the madonna blue *I. histrioides* Major, and a lot of snowdrops. The winter prunus and winter jasmine can be picked on a one-minute sortie from the house.

Luckily, the evergreen rubbish which is traditional for Christmas, the holly and the Christmas tree, can be confined to your house, for you like them in their season, and I have a primeval horror of them, especially the conifers.

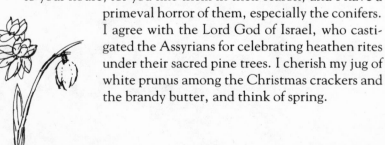

I agree with the Lord God of Israel, who castigated the Assyrians for celebrating heathen rites under their sacred pine trees. I cherish my jug of white prunus among the Christmas crackers and the brandy butter, and think of spring.

Catalogues

Dear C,

Bad news, our favourite garden centre has changed hands. True, it was becoming increasingly a fun fair, with its aquarium, slides for kiddies, thatched wendy houses, lollipop dispensers and other non-horticultural attractions, but even so, the plants were well grown and often unusual. I once bought a *Rosa filipes* Kiftsgate there, and a very beautiful pyramidal crab apple called Everest which I have not seen elsewhere. The two proprietors became friends of mine and often helped me choose plants of real worth, with a proper complement of roots, when they found me foolishly counting the buds. Now I fear it will cater for the lowest common denominator.

However, this disappointment gives me a chance to persuade you to think less of buying plants in a supermarket spirit and to take a look at some catalogues. There is a certain pleasure which I share with you in instant shopping, perhaps fancying a shrub in a pot and planting it within the hour, but this is not gardening. Gardening means planning and choosing the best, perhaps studying several dictionaries and catalogues before deciding on a plant and then, probably, ordering by post. (Bedding plants are an exception, best chosen in the flesh and planted out as quickly as possible, unless you have the facilities for growing them from seed.)

Catalogues are a delightful form of garden literature. I don't mean the garish bulb catalogues with hideous colour photographs of giant hyacinths which list very few varieties and are inaccurate as to names – the Dutch, who perpetrate most of these nasty brochures, don't seem to know any Latin. But the connoisseur's catalogues, usually in black and white, sometimes with first-rate sketches and typography, make ideal fireside reading. Here you will find, not four or five different apple trees, but many dozens, each listed with a description of its height, shape, colour of blossom and fruiting time, so that each has a personality. There are even apples which do not ripen until December or January, though I have not tried them. In the herbaceous world, there are enticing catalogues of unusual and variegated plants, and there are small nurseries in various parts of Britain, particularly in the north, specialising in such nostalgic delights as double primroses and old-fashioned pansies.

I will get a few catalogues for you and hope to get you hooked.

February

Latin Names

Dear Clare,

I think we had better have the battle about Latin names sooner rather than later, and it won't take me long to have you on the ropes.

I know you like my hellebores and talk of growing some yourself. Are you going to write to a nursery and order 'six hellebores please'? I don't know what you would get. I have in my garden *Helleborus atrorubens*, with blood-red cup-shaped flowers which come out at Christmas, *H. orientalis* in many colours, with speckles inside the petals and which flowers for weeks from early spring, *H. foetidus*, a glorious evergreen with clusters of pale green flowers which seeds all over the garden, bless it, *H. corsicus*, a larger plant with flowers like pale green water-lilies, and *H. cyclophyllus*, a rarer plant which was given to me by a great botanist, Chris Brickell. He collected it in the Pindus mountains in Greece, where I would give my soul to see it growing wild.

I also have the native (i.e. it is an English wild plant) *H. viridis*, but thereby hangs a moral tale. Years ago, I dug up a small piece in a local wood, importing with the soil the seeds of a horrible woodland weed, Dog's Mercury, which spreads remorselessly and which I have never been able to eradicate. I broke the rules and nature took revenge.

The hellebores are not a large genus, but when I tell you that there are thousands of species of euphorbia, of which I grow perhaps a dozen, you will see that identification must be exact. Even 'honeysuckle' will not do to describe a plant except in literature and casual conversation, for there are many honeysuckles. Are you thinking of the wild *Lonicera periclymenum* which twines round your garden table in the form Serotina? Or of the rampant evergreen *L. japonica* Halliana which grows over your porch, giving out an overpowering scent? Or of *L. fragrantissima*, which is a shrub, not a climber, and begins to flower in late winter? Or of the honeysuckle with rosy red flowers, *L. italica*, which smothers the old stump of the once splendid prunus tree in my garden which a weekend guest (meaning well) trimmed and killed by mistake?

Have I made my case? When serious gardeners gather together, Latin names are essential. English names are baby-talk.

Dear Mater,

On the ropes and gasping. The most I achieved at school in the way of Latin was a couple of sentences about the farmers adorning the tables with roses, and I don't suppose that will do. For now, I may have to stick to, 'That's a nice hellebore' and 'Do you do it in red?' and I shall avoid any parties where all these serious gardeners are boozing. This particular problem could be a difficult one to crack, so please bear with me. You have coped with my academic inadequacies for so long now, I expect you'll manage for a bit longer.

Lilies

Dearest C,

I am nervous of the spectacular in simple cottage gardens like yours and mine, but I make an exception for lilies. Many of them are hardy and easy to grow and at least one of them, the madonna lily, has been a cottage plant for centuries. Therefore I will make your mouth water with the enclosed catalogue which has just arrived from de Jager, the bulb firm, which is full of luscious pictures of lilies plain, striped or spotted, trumpet-shaped or with recurved petals, for planting between now and April or, if you miss this boat, in the autumn.

The instructions in the catalogue are so clear that I will not repeat them – good drainage, crumbly soil rich in humus, lots of peat, regular watering, though I think the growers are a little optimistic as to the number of lilies which will thrive in limy soil. Those which will not, like the glorious *Lilium auratum*, do better in pots filled with a peaty compost, and you could grow them on your roof garden in London. As a rule of thumb, beware of American or Japanese lilies in a limy garden, and choose lilies from West China or from countries round the Mediterranean, such as Greece or Asia Minor.

In your cottage garden I would start with the easiest of all lilies, *L. regale* from Tibet, which will grow anywhere, a tall, white lily with large trumpet flowers with yellow in the throat and purplish shading on the outside. They have large golden anthers which spill their pollen on your clothes, but luckily it washes out. I had a group once in my garden in the bed under the Bramley apple tree, and it spread like a weed for several years, then it died away. This is apt to happen with lilies and it is no good making a fuss, one must plant a new lot in another place.

Oddly enough, the cottage or madonna lily is not as easy to grow as it used to be – pictures of Victorian cottage gardens are usually full of the plant – and for a second easy choice I suggest the extra tall *L. henryi*, which flowers in August and has orange-yellow flowers which nod their heads. A clump by the front door would impress the troops. Being a mountain flower by nature, like many lilies, it is very hardy. If you want lilies in your copse by the boundary hedge, try a few martagon lilies; these have comparatively small flowers, but plenty of them, they like a little shade and increase in a satisfactory manner. You can get them in pink, purple or white.

Windbreaks

Dearest child,

You probably know only too well that your garden is very windy, though not as exposed as mine, and that you must choose fully hardy plants for places which catch the south-wester, which is more damaging than even the east wind in your particular position. I know you were disappointed when the scented white jasmine (*Jasminum officinale*) which you planted on the trellis round your outdoor dining-table failed, burned up by the wind, but luckily the honeysuckle with which you replaced it looks healthy and should take the exposure.

Lots of plants which are perfectly hardy as far as frost goes don't like the wind – roses, in particular, can be rocked almost out of the soil – so try to put these in protected places and, looking to the future, plant some tough, windproof shrubs in strategic spots to create shelter. The beautiful old lilacs which you inherited are a gift as shelter plants, and you could plant something more delicate, like daphnes, in their lee. Lilacs don't look great when they are not in flower, but they serve this purpose well. Yours seem to grow on their own roots (they have not been grafted) and therefore do not sucker, which is the curse of my dark purple lilac called, I think, Black Night. The suckers bear anaemic mauve flowers.

Another good shelter shrub (don't throw up your hands in horror) is common laurel, *Prunus laurocerasus*. Common it is when grown as a clipped hedge, but an unpruned bush is a handsome plant with fine spikes of flower, and very protec-tive. Also, if it is your fate, as it used to be mine, to be on the church flower roster for January, it will provide you with some winter branches showy enough to compete with that unfortunate reredos. Incidentally, my hellebores seem to thrive in the shadow of a laurel.

I hope we can have a lot of barbecue meals in your

honeysuckle-girt dining space this summer. I will bring my own cubes of lamb as your pork kebabs, though tasty, give me indigestion. I fear I am turning into the importunate granny in *After Henry*, and you are not unlike her daughter, Prunella Scales, in character, the highest compliment I could pay you.

A Small Tree

Dear Clare,

You have been musing for some time about a tree to break up the *ennui* of that sloping stretch of grass behind your cottage, but you haven't taken action. If you really want one, and I think you do, it ought to go in at once. The right choice is crucial, for your tree will be a companion for life.

It would be creative to plant a forest tree, a chestnut or a beech for those hereafter, but, apart from your understandable impatience, I don't think there is enough space, so it will have to be a small tree growing up to, say, sixteen feet.

This sounds snobbish, but I would avoid anything banal which you see in every other garden, or any tree which is pretty for a mere week or two when in blossom; this applies to many prunuses, though some compensate by making autumn colour. My first thought is for a weeping tree, not a giant weeping willow which would undermine your cottage, but perhaps a weeping ash or willow-leaved pear. If you were on sandy soil I would suggest a weeping birch, such as *Betula pendula* Youngii, which is a charmer, but is not ideal for chalk.

If, however, you do not want a weeper, but a tree with a spreading head to sit under, it is hard to beat *Malus floribunda*, an ornamental apple of mushroom shape with red and white blossom – you would have to strip the trunk of its lower branches, but this improves many trees, letting in light on the ground beneath. It is important to know that a prunus should be stripped only in late summer, but a malus could be pruned at almost any time, although best in spring; cut no more than one or two branches a month, to avoid shock to the tree. You cut each branch back to the 'shoulder' where it joins the trunk, never cut into the trunk itself, and then rub the wound with damp earth. (Wound paint is no longer recommended.) Another choice for your tree might be an edible crab apple, which would give you blossom in spring

and a crop of doll's-house apples in autumn. The prettiest
fruit, being orange flushed with red, and the best for jelly,
grows on the John Downie variety, but Golden Hornet
makes a better shaped tree.

Then one must think about the sorbus family. If your soil
were neutral, I would strongly press for a rowan, or mountain
ash, most of which have beautiful ferny leaves which colour
in autumn and set off the hanging bunches of scarlet fruit,
but it would be risky on chalk. But another sorbus, the
whitebeam (*Sorbus aucuparia*), loves chalk and grows wild in
our district. In spring, the silvery young leaves grow in
cup-shaped clusters like magnolia blossoms, but they go a bit
dry and crumply in autumn. The species in my garden, *S.
aria* Lutescens, does not have a natural mushroom head, but
if you stripped the lower branches it would give enough
shade to sit under. My largest specimen does in fact make a
perfect sun umbrella because once during a storm there were
blue flashes when the uppermost branches struck some
overhead wires and the electricity company hurried round
and cut off the top of the tree. The men did it skilfully and by
a miracle improved the tree, though not the scenery. 'How
nice, it has opened up the wirescape,' John Betjeman told
me brutally.

You must hurry if you want to plant your tree this year,
otherwise we could do some garden visiting in the summer
and choose a tree to plant next winter. You will have to shop
quickly if you want a tree now and I suggest a session on the
telephone to some tree nurseries, and if you find what you
want you will save time by going to collect it. I will help you
plant your tree, whatever it is, you and Nick doing the work
while I stand by giving maddening advice.

Planting Your Tree

Dear C,

Osbert and I once stayed for several days with a great gardener called Princess Sturdza. She has a magnificent woodland garden on the cliffs of Normandy near Dieppe and I had gone to write about it. We dined every evening with the family, but foraged for ourselves for lunch, trying out one local restaurant after another. Osbert revelled in this part of the expedition and said sagely, 'Always make for the restaurant with plenty of French cars outside, especially if you can spot the mayoral limousine and discover where his worship has his lunch'. Failing this, he would look for tables laid with napkins in rings, 'a sure sign of regular satisfied customers'. The result was that we feasted every day in inconspicuous little places with superlative Normandy food and no tourists. It was very fattening.

But back to business. Princess Sturdza, showing me her methods with trees, said 'spend three sous on the plant and thirty sous on the planting', which is apparently an old French adage, the French being, I believe, the greatest of all nations for forestry. She added, 'Remember you will be giving your tree its home for life.'

So strip a very large circle in your turf and dig a very large hole, breaking up the sub-soil, but not bringing it to the surface. Then dig in some well-rotted manure, which I can provide from my two-year-old heap, and add some damp peat. Then put a strong stake in the hole *before you plant*, then put in your tree, treading the soil down firmly, then tie it to the stake – the latest theory is to attach tree to stake low down, a couple of feet from the ground, though it seems more logical to tie it high up; but the idea is that the tree will learn to rely on its own roots if it is not given too much help. The most modern experts advise you not to stake at all, on the same sort of principle now applied in hospitals – you long to have your broken bone strapped up, but they leave the two halves to scrunch until they knit on their own. In my windy garden, however, young trees will continue to be staked. You will have to water the soil round your tree copiously this summer, and for several summers afterwards.

Planting a tree is definitely a two-person job, one to hold the tree in a perfectly upright position while the other shoves in the soil – even roses I find difficult to plant on my own. Life must have been pleasant for an old-fashioned head gardener, who always had a 'boy' to call on for the donkey work, the boy often being a gnarled old chap who had not risen in his profession. It is miraculous how much the single-handed gardener achieves today, for machinery is not the answer for tasks which want sensitive handling.

March

Rose Pruning

Dear C,

This will be a stodgy letter, the subject being too solemn for frivolity. We should both start pruning our roses now. When to prune which roses is a tricky question, as the experts differ, and so do the roses. Some roses, notably hybrid teas and floribunda or cluster roses, like your Iceberg, flower on the new wood which should spring forth abundantly after pruning. Others flower on the old wood (the shoots which grew last year) and need different treatment.

The first kind should be pruned now though some experts, including the great Fred Whitsey, recommend earlier pruning, even as early as January. (I would be nervous of this except in a mild district like Cornwall.) I used to cut my cluster roses back very hard, down to the fifth bud on every stem, but they took so long to recover that it was late summer before I got any flowers. I suggest a lighter pruning, just shaping the bushes neatly and cutting off lanky, straggling stems. All dead wood must go. At the same time, give the bushes a rose feed which you buy by the bag at the garden shop. *And spray for blackspot.*

Roses which flower on the old wood, such as climbers and ramblers, and many shrub roses, like the gallicas, should be pruned after flowering in late summer or autumn to allow the maximum time for new wood to shoot and ripen. My pink-and-white striped gallica, Rosa Mundi, flowered so prodigiously last July that I had to clip it over with shears. I know that you did, correctly, prune your climbers in the autumn, but look them over again and cut off any die-back, making a slanting cut just above a bud.

Why are your roses better than mine? It is very annoying. The fact is that mine have gone downhill. Years ago, people used to stop their cars to admire the Albertine on the house, and the little rose garden was so floriferous with Iceberg and Rosemary Rose that it was photographed in the RHS

Journal. Now the plants are old and you might think it would be sensible to replace them, but the problem goes deeper than that. *All my roses need re-siting.* Of course I know that you cannot plant new roses in an old rose bed without changing the soil to a depth of about 2 feet, but I have tried that and it doesn't work. I think that roses get tired of the air they breathe as well as of the soil they grow in, and they need new quarters.

But how can I afford to move my rose garden, with its cobbled paving and box edging? And where would it go? And how could I bear to strip the front of the cottage of the climbing roses which, though past their best, do look quite charming in June and July? I am rather depressed about this.

However, I enjoy the sight of that glorious old bourbon on the front of your cottage which nobody has been able to name, though Great Western is the best suggestion so far. And for some immoral reason your Icebergs, badly placed under apple trees, thrive in the teeth of all the rules. Bother.

Dear M,

Thank you for your encyclopaedic letter on rose pruning, but I am an incompetent calendar gardener and am taking up Nick's theory of pruning. *In the spring hack it back.*

This practice has in fact worked rather well with the various roses which each year look better and better. I'm glad you have noticed the Iceberg, which flowered ceaselessly last year. Nick will be gratified, too, as he thought you were rather crisp about his efforts. He likes to prune, so please do not discourage him. I do agree, however, that the Nick theory did not work in connection with the blackcurrant bushes – not a single berry last year. Personally, I didn't mind much as I still have three jars of jam labelled 1986.

But I have other rose problems. I can't cure the old roses on the front of the cottage of blackspot. Any schemes? I spray and spray but still they erupt in one giant spot per leaf, almost while I am looking at them. This quite puts me off them, and the blooms themselves look rather damp and mildewed round the edges. Every year you admire them, and I do too at the beginning of the season, but by the end of the summer I am in despair. Sometimes I am quite tempted to do away with them, and plant some nice modern germ-free roses, which seem to come bristling with green and glossy leaves. I feed them quite a lot, although I never have much confidence in the amount they suggest on the packet. It doesn't seem nearly enough, so where they recommend two ounces I usually shovel on about eight.

I would like to plant a new rose over the rustic pole porch. It can replace the rather uninteresting honeysuckle which refuses to grow. Did you once suggest a rose called Aloha? I looked for it in the garden centre without success. Don't tell me – back to the catalogues.

By the way, people still stop to look at the roses on the front of your house, so take heart.

Pillar Roses

Dearest C,

You raised a lot of different topics in your last letter, so I will pick on roses only this time. I must say first, because it cannot wait, that you are quite mad to play about with the instructions on gardening packets. Whether the product is a food or a poison, it has been formulated by scientists who may not be enchanting conversationalists or Renaissance men living the rounded life, but who know their iron chelate from their aminotriazole. It is literally dangerous to be your own chemist.

But for a rose for your rustic porch: strictly you want a 'pillar rose', which means a climber of moderate ambitions, and preferably one with flexible branches which are easy to train. Look in the catalogues for roses of not more than 10 or at most 12 feet, preferably modern roses which are less likely to get the dreaded blackspot than the beloved old ones.

Handel is a strong contender, if you do not object to bicolour roses; it grows to 12 feet, the cream-and-pink double flowers coming in a gratifyingly long succession. Of the dark red roses, Guinée is probably the best for your purpose. The flowers are like red velvet and give out one of the sweetest scents in the rose garden. I am a bit nervous of yellow roses on chalk, for I suspect that some do not like lime, but if you care to risk it Golden Showers is a celebrated pillar rose growing to only 7 feet. The New Dawn, of a delicate shell-pink with a lovely scent, would, I think, be too vigorous for your porch, but it has a smaller progeny, the Aloha you mention, which would probably be the best choice of all. It grows to 8 feet, is nearly perpetual, and has large double deep pink scented flowers which do not get mildew. Yes, make it Guinée or Aloha.

When planting a pillar rose, whether on a fence, screen, pergola, wall or, in your case, a porch, plant it close to the support and train it from the early days, with as many branches as possible stretching out horizontally. These will get the benefit of extra sunshine and will 'break' into more flowering shoots than will a vertical branch. Roses are flowers of the sun, and although a number of roses will do well on a north wall, they would probably do even better on a south wall. Mme Alfred Carrière is often recommended as a rose which will accept shade, and so it will, but I have never seen it so smothered with flowers as on the wall of the South Cottage at Sissinghurst, where it faces slightly west of south.

Let us plan now to have an outing at the end of June to the National Trust Garden at Mottisfont Abbey in Hampshire to see the huge collection of roses planted by Graham Stuart Thomas. It is only an hour's drive, and we could take a picnic.

Fast Food

Dear Calypso,

Here is a packet of French Breakfast radish seed, a very pretty radish which is red at the top and white towards the root. Sow them now *very thinly*, and water them well if the soil seems dry. I will help you thin them if they come up crowded too closely together, when you will get a lot of green leaves and no radishes. With luck, you will have bread-and-butter with radishes for tea in about four weeks – please invite me. Or you could serve them in a saucer as an appetizer with Coca-Cola.

I will get you some seed of Giant Sunflower this week which will grow taller than Mummy or even Granny, and the flowers will have enormous amiable faces.

Goodbye, Garden

Darling Clare,

I am overwhelmed with the deep melancholia which always attacks me when I am about to travel. I look round the garden as though I were seeing it for the last time. I feel like Bette Davis in *Dark Victory*, bravely planting hyacinths though blind and about to die of a tumour on the brain, both disabilities unnoticed by her husband. (Would Osbert have noticed? Probably not.)

As you know, I am leaving for Jordan tomorrow, with good companions, Petra in sight, they tell me the weather is perfect. I am going for a mere ten days and have been looking forward to it madly. But idiotic angst claws me.

I will not even be missing much here. I have seen the daffodils in their glorious prime, the *Scilla bithynica* is out, the primroses and *Anemone blanda* make yellow and blue carpets; all I am going to miss are the crown imperials, and they may hold until my return if the weather stays chilly. So what am I blithering about? Even if the cottage burns down, the garden will still be left, give or take a charred shrub or two. As soon as I am airborne I will feel elated. Pre-travel blues is, to me, like premenstrual tension (from which luckily I never suffered) to other women.

I must go and pack. Happy gardening, love to Calypso, Max, Charlie *et al*, from your mother on her way to the scaffold, i.e. Gatwick.

April

Lilies of the Field

Darling C,

It is paradise here, cloudless weather, a programme of antiquities to see, including Petra, and such wild flowers as I have never dreamed of. Red anemones even push up in waste places in the city of Amman, and there are orchids outside the hotel.

This country makes me feel that I only like flowers wild. The soil is very rich and the crops unsprayed, so that every field and wayside verge is massed with flowers. Purple gladioli are weeds in the cornfields, the Black Iris which I had never even heard of before springs out of stony clefts, red anemones and marigolds and tiny blue irises and white hollyhocks grow in masses all over the country.

I have had great difficulty in identifying the flowers as there is no Field Guide to the area, and only a few of the species are the same as those of the Mediterranean. But I think the gladiolus, a graceful flower which shames its hideous stiff relatives sold in English flower shops, is G. *atroviolaceus*, and the red anemone, which is thought to be the biblical 'lilies of the field', is A. *coronaria*, and the iris with the large black flower-head is I. *nigricans*. But I haven't found the hollyhock yet, nor many of the others, and I am going to throw myself on Anthony Huxley's mercy when I get home, showing him some of the photographs which Cara is taking.

It all takes me back to where I began in my childhood; it was an early love of wild flowers which led me into gardening. I now feel that all I want is a wild garden, quite unplanned, where flowers will seed and seed. I never want to see a herbaceous border, a knot garden, or even a rose garden again.

This is, of course, nonsense, because a wild garden only looks beautiful in the spring. I am told that in a week or two from now it will get really hot here and the whole country will dry up. In England, where the spring lasts longer, wild flowers can be enjoyed for months, but without organised planting in the garden there would be little to look at in summer and autumn. When I get home, I will recover my sanity.

Talking of lilies of the field, the New English Bible has 'And why be anxious about clothes?' for 'And why take ye thought for raiment?', as though a nervous executive's wife was worrying about what to wear to the office party.

Garden Open Today

Dearest C,

Now that the 'garden open' season has begun, we might try to visit a famous garden now and again on a Saturday or Sunday. These trips do open the eyes. Not that I think for a moment that you *ought* to do this, for you work so hard in the week that you deserve duty-free weekends, and by the time you have taken Calypso for a ride, entertained a friend or two, and probably included me in Sunday lunch, there's not much time left. As for Calypso, I never knew a child who was so rarely at a loose end. But we might have a sample outing, perhaps to a garden where we can get a cream tea. If Calypso doesn't enjoy it, we could abandon her next time and dump her at the ever-hospitable Higleys; she likes bossing Rebecca about.

Garden visiting is now as popular a national pastime as football but without the danger of yobboes and riots. Personally, I go partly for the aesthetic pleasure, but also to learn about plants and design, and to loot from the plant stall, where there are often unusual plants for sale which are difficult to find in commercial centres.

On a long trip, I equip myself with maps and guidebooks and a picnic lunch, but our first expeditions would be in the neighbourhood – perhaps to the Old Rectory at Farnborough where dear Betjeman once lived. The garden was a wild place in those days, largely a scratching ground for Penelope's caponned chickens which were the size of turkeys. (She doctored them herself.) Today there are masses of old roses and fine herbaceous borders and an elegant swimming pool which Betj would not have cared for.

The secret of getting more out of a garden visit than an 'oo-er, isn't it lovely' experience is to go round at least twice. I go round the first time to enjoy myself and to get an overall idea of the garden, and the second time I take a lot of notes and make crude sketches, because unless you have a marvellous visual memory you forget what you have seen. How well a patch of autumn cyclamen looks under a pine tree, thriving in the carpet of needles . . . the yellow-flowered *Clematis tangutica* shows up well trained through an evergreen, per-haps an elaeagnus . . . seeds of candytuft can be scattered successfully in paving cracks, and come up in cottagey clumps (must tell Calypso) . . . whatever the price, I must have more box. Colour groupings can be inspiring, too, such as black tulips with forget-me-nots, instead of boring pink ones; or white flowers with apricot, such as white roses underplanted with alstroemerias. If I carry out one idea in twenty it is a miracle, for I am short of many resources, and my garden is too thickly planted as it is, but seeing perfection gives one goals to strive for.

Let us look up the National Gardens Scheme yellow guide and fix a date. We won't go at opening time, but later, when the light will be softer. Gardens look their worst at mid-day when the sun is garish and the shadows are hard.

Pink and Yellow

Dear Clare,

Because the winter has been mild, all the spring flowers in my garden have come out together and it does look gratifyingly like a sentimental Victorian cottage picture. But there is one nasty colour clash which jars – there are two trees flowering with pink blossom with sheets of daffodils underneath. Years ago, I planted in the front garden a *Prunus cerasifera* Pissardii, or purple-leaved plum, which is not my favourite prunus now, and the pink flowers and purple leaves are too gaudy for the March Sunshine daffodils below. And the clash happens again in the orchard where I have a bright pink form of *Prunus subhirtella* which coincides with the early Tenby daffodils.

If I were starting again, I would choose such pink-flowered trees as do not bloom until May, when the daffodils are over – apple blossom springs to mind – and I would plant trees with white blossom to canopy the daffodils. Of these, the double gean is superb, a double form of the English wild cherry, and of the Japanese prunuses, I would love to have *P. Shirotae*, with spreading branches loaded with bunches of large semi-double white flowers.

There was one in Eaton Square which the London pigeons used to disbud systematically, pecking the buds and dropping them to the ground, and I could have murdered Mrs Elmer who used to feed these disgusting birds on her way home from hoovering and polishing our flat. I used to say, 'Mrs E, you are *not* to use my bread for feeding vermin,' but she regularly sneaked out with a paper bag full of crusts. Incidentally, I got a card from her in Australia the other day, still very legibly written, saying she had moved into a home where they play bingo every evening and she had never been happier. I have written her a long letter with heavily censored news of you and Max.

But back to naturalised daffodils, of which a careless initial choice can never be corrected. In my salad days I planted the orchard with a glorious mixture of trumpets, dwarfs, jonquils, long cups, short cups and so on, all bought cheap as a job lot, and now they have spread into motley sheets, flowering at different times. Yours, with a different variety under each tree, including the white Dove Wings, look much prettier.

Garden Snobbery

Dear Clare,

I confess to being a garden snob, as you will be, too, with a bit more experience. Let me explain this. I have no special admiration for the gardens of the aristocracy, some of which are beautiful, others not. Still less do I value money-power in any department of life, and the gardens of the very rich are often the worst. But I *am* snobbish about the banal, and when I see a planting which is so frequently used as to be utterly boring, I want to avoid it. The common dismissive word for such planting is 'suburban', but this is unfair to the suburbs, which are inhabited by some of the best gardeners in Britain. The word has taken off because sometimes all the gardeners in a street or district tend to copy one another, and you see the same Kanzan cherry trees, the same camellias, the same hybrid tea roses repeated until they become a cliché. I think that my objection to my pink prunus with daffodils is of snobbish rather than aesthetic origin. They might look well together if one saw this combination of pastels for the first time.

Many good plants and plant associations which were yesterday's fashion seem to snobs like me to be a bit down-market today. Take the bright pink Queen Elizabeth rose, a fine rose in itself, with a well-shaped flower and strong scent, but now so commonplace that it is scarcely worth a second glance. I would rather plant a hybrid musk like Buff Beauty or Felicia, more subtle in colour, for lasting pleasure. Then I cannot abide dwarf conifers springing out of a bed of heathers, which look like a catalogue picture rather than a natural garden scene, as does a rock garden with a waterfall on a flat site. It is usually first-time gardeners who adopt these copycat features, instead of thinking for themselves, and they look awful in the wrong background. They are heartily disliked by the old-timers in our village, and 'expensive eyesores' is an expression I have heard used in the pub.

I am even doubtful about laburnum tunnels, so appropriate in magnificent scenic gardens like Bodnant. But a little tunnel leading from nowhere to nowhere seems pretentious, and may be despised in a few years' time, like yesterday's fashion of a Dorothy Perkins rose over a trellis arch.

So I defend garden snobbery if it makes you use your own eyes instead of copying fashionable ideas. I remember a television programme on which a needling interviewer asked Nancy Mitford, heroine of U and non-U, 'Don't you think you are a bit of a snob?' She answered, 'Of course I am, aren't you?', thus neatly turning the tables.

Pruning Shrubs

Dear C,

This is going to be stodgy letter number 2, I'm afraid, for I ought to remind you that some shrubs should now be pruned, and since this is not a romantic or evocative subject, I'll try to be brief.

Many spring and early summer shrubs flower on last year's growth of wood, and you should prune them as soon as they have flowered to allow them nearly a year to make new shoots and buds. So prune now your winter jasmine (if you haven't already done it), your forsythia and your *Mahonia japonica*. The jasmine and forsythia are easy, just cut two-thirds off all the shoots which have flowered. Your mahonia may not need pruning and many gardeners do not realise that it *can* be pruned, but as yours is getting a bit sprawly I would cut some of the longer branches just above a bud. The bud will suddenly turn into a promising shoot.

Looking forward a month or two, deadhead your lilac *immediately* after flowering, or it will waste its energy in making seeds and you will get only a few flowers next year, and cut back the faded shoots of your deutzia and *Spiraea arguta*, a laborious job, as the flowering shoots of these thickety bushes can be counted in hundreds. Do the same with the philadelphus in late June or July, or whenever the heavenly blossom is finished. They will look bare at first, but new shoots will soon fill the gaps.

Some of the hedges should be clipped now, the first on the list being lavender. Box can wait until midsummer, and yew until August.

But not all shrubs are the better for pruning, and *Mahonia aquifolium*, some hydrangeas and many viburnums can be left alone for years. When in doubt, I implore you to look up your *Reader's Digest Encyclopaedia*.

I have always been an ardent pruner, and now that working on all fours is agony, thanks to my decrepit knees, it is enjoyable to have a job which one can carry out standing on two legs, like the pigs in *Animal Farm*.

My preferred pruning tool is secateurs, though many gardeners use a pruning knife with a curved handle. I like orange- or yellow-handled secateurs, as I leave them all over the garden, and they are easily found. Shears, of course, are essential for hedges, a small saw for solid branches, and long-handled parrot-bill secateurs for lofty shrubs, such as lilac, though these are top-heavy and brutes to handle. All pruning tools must be really sharp, or you will get torn cuts, which are ugly and may invite disease.

Wisteria

Dearest Clare,

What an exciting weekend! The first flower-buds on your wisteria, and you haven't had to wait the traditional seven years, you say it's only four. I do congratulate you, your wisteria clearly likes you. It looks wonderfully green and healthy. I cannot wait for those rough acorn-like buds to lengthen into hanging flowers.

Your wisteria is probably a descendant of two small plants which were sent to Britain from Canton in 1816. Apparently a Chinese merchant called Consequa gave them to British friends who sent them home. I think the story must be authentic because when Consequa died he was awarded an obituary in *The Times*.

You often accuse me of being beastly to Nick about his gardening, but I do think he is training the wisteria beautifully, and I can imagine it very soon weaving round the windows and climbing to the thatch. Your plant is still too young to need much pruning, though some of the new tendrils might be cut off in summer when it has flowered. Mature plants are given their main pruning in winter, each shoot being cut back to two or three buds.

Garden Poem

Dear Granny,

I have written a poem for you about my garden and have typed it on your typewriter. I hope you will like it.

How the Garden Grows
In my garden grows a sweet little rose,
    I planted her with lots of care,
I'll tell you what I did,
    I got some bulbs and my trowel,
I started digging,
    Mud was flinging,
I stoped digging,
    Mud stoped flinging.
I put the bulbs in very well.
I covered them as well as I could,
and that is how my rose stood.

I replied: Dear Calypso,
Thank you very much for the poem. I agree with you that planting things is a most satisfactory feeling. If you will get the ground ready, I will give you a rose to plant. It may not have a bulb at the end, but it will have plenty of roots.

Dear M,

Don't rush to buy the rose for Calypso. Her enthusiasm for formal digging seems to be on the wane. The little rock garden which was her pride and joy last year seems to have fallen into my hands to maintain. After digging for all of a minute last weekend she tossed her fork aside and announced that she didn't think 'gardening was quite her thing'. What she really means is that she can't bear to tackle it on her own. Calypso likes to have me beside her doing most of the work while she looks on commenting the while on what I'm doing wrong. But she derives a lot of fun out of your greenhouse, or the 'laboratory' as it is now known, and I don't think you'll be allowed in yourself unless you know the password.

In case you didn't know it, you also have a secret 'camp' area at the bottom of your garden. Quite a lot of digging has gone on there, and strange unidentified seeds have been scattered all over the place. Calypso and friend Becky also decorated the trees with flowers while you were away. Lots of them. Daffodil heads, primrose heads, forget-me-not heads, were all laid along the tree branches 'to make them look prettier'.

Your garden was not the only hit area, mine too. The little vandals were quite surprised at my reaction; they are very chastened now. Don't be alarmed at the headless stalks you may spot from time to time, it's not a new pest sent to try you, merely the old one.

Just Three Rows

Dear Clare,

Once upon a time, when you were small and gardeners were cheap and my knees were in good working order, I had a proper vegetable garden and even beds of soft fruit – strawberries, raspberries, gooseberries and currants. Gradually, as wages went up and my physique went down, the vegetable garden contracted and has now, as you know, gone altogether. You, sensibly, have never started one.

But if I could manage it, I would like to grow just three rows of such vegetables as can never be bought in top condition in the shops, and I would choose broad beans, runner beans, and a row divided between Little Gem cos lettuces, Little Marvel peas, and sorrel. Shop beans and peas are always large and tough and lettuces never seem quite fresh – as they have often come from half way across the world, it is not surprising. Sorrel is a wonderful plant, permanent, evergreen, hardy, always there to pick for sorrel soup and sauces.

I find many shop vegetables first class, including asparagus (Osbert would often drop hints about an asparagus bed, but I'm afraid he never got it); and sprouts, celery and cabbages are better grown commercially than by the private gardener unless he has infinite time. Onions and tomatoes do better, I think, in sunny Spain than rainy England. But just a few home-grown veg are a treat and one day you may be tempted. I wonder what your choice for 'just three rows' would be, perhaps not the same as mine.

We both grow herbs, of course, and this year I plan to extend my parsley bed, for one cannot have too much parsley and you are always stealing mine. Connoisseurs favour the flat-leaved French parsley, but I am quite happy with Moss Curled.

If one has enough parsley one can make parsley soup, which I first tasted when staying with foodie Quentin Crewe, who had a superlative cook. You need very good chicken stock, slightly thickened, which you heat and then stir in masses and masses of parsley chopped very small, and cook it for three minutes. The soup is bright green and parsley is the predominant taste, rather than being just a garnish. (It is decent of me to tell you this, but a couple of tins of Vichysoisse are as good as the stock. In exchange, would you consider giving me your exclusive recipe for courgettes with parsley and cream? They are delicious.)

Parsley can be troublesome to germinate, especially in a late spring if the soil is cold. You can water the bed with hot water before sowing, but even so I think it is wise to make three sowings at three-week intervals, and at least one is sure to come through.

Dear M,

I did attempt a few veggies once. Not a success, I'm afraid. For a start I began from seed, sowing directly into the bed. String was in short supply that weekend so they came up in wiggly rows, which was unsatisfying. Also Porridge had a puppyish way of scratching up the seeds – wretched animal!

A vegetable patch seems to me to be the one area where everything should be rigorously regimented. I love to see opulent lines of fat beans leading smartly on to a line of onions. My lettuces grew a treat but we never found time to eat them all and they went to seed. Since then I have converted the patch to sweet peas which have been a triumph. In fact, they are always a lot better than yours, so now I take a smug pride in devoting a lot of energy to them. Never were plants more lavishly tended. The bed is regularly manured (from your heap), their tendrils lovingly severed, and from

day one they are bound St Joan fashion to their stakes. I
terrify them into growth. Any hints you would like about
this, you only have to ask.

I also love my herb bed, it increases in size every year. It
occupies the best space in the garden, sheltered by the hedge
and in full sun. I tried a bit of topiary on the chives this
weekend, copying the way you use chives as a mini clipped
hedge around the herb border. A certain amount of grass has
inveigled its way into the centre of some of my clumps, but I
don't think it matters much; with all the other foodie
pollution to worry about I put grass about last on the agenda.

Kind Words

Dearest C,

I have been thinking this weekend about Osbert's contribution to the garden, and really he was a most destructive gardener. True, he sometimes pruned the roses (surprisingly well), and occasionally clipped the box hedges in the front garden (predictably badly), leaving a saddleback depression in the middle of each. He also ruined several beds by introducing rampant plants from his much larger garden at Henley, notably the *Acanthus spinosus* which has swamped various clematis and done in some good nerines.

But he made an enormous contribution in the way of encouragement. He never saw the weeds, only the flowers, and every time we went round the garden he would say, 'Darling, I do congratulate you', and mean it.

He also adored our outdoor meals at the slate table, though he carried not so much as a fork from the house, nor took back a single dirty plate. He liked the table properly laid as by a parlour-maid, and at least two courses and Turkish coffee, all of which he got. Goodness, he was spoiled. The coffee, incidentally, I always served in the tiny coffee cups which we bought in a remote mountain village at the end of a terrifying hairpin road in northern Greece, thinking them pleasantly ethnic, only to find when we got home that they were marked 'Made in Japan'.

Pasha and slave we were, but as there is no human quality which adds so much to life as a capacity for enjoyment, at which Osbert shone, the slave was willing. Today, I have to garden for myself alone, and I do not like it. I get more fun out of watching you creating your garden, which has a future rather than a past.

Lime Green

Dear Clare,

Almost my favourite colour is yellow with a dash of green in it, the yellow of a lemon which is not quite ripe. This weekend I am revelling in my single yellow peonies, *Paeonia mlokosewitschii*, commonly known as 'Mlok', a peony from the Causasus with large yellow stamens crowded inside the flower cups. We must try to get a piece from my garden into yours in the autumn. I grew mine from seed given me by the novelist H.E. Bates, who was an outstanding gardener but rather a mean man. I went from London to Kent years ago to write a feature on his garden, and we spent several enjoyable hours discussing the garden and its plants, at the end of which I longed for, but didn't get, a cup of tea – amazing how these trifles rankle. Bates told me the seeds would flower after five years, which they did to the day.

The flowers are fleeting, but as the young leaves are an exciting red in early spring and colour again in autumn, there is more mileage in this peony than you might expect. It has also what are called 'interesting' seedpods, but seedpods are an advanced taste which I have not yet acquired.

Another, but little-known, lime-green plant is *Smyrnium perfoliatum* (no English name), with greeny-yellow umbel-liferous flowers wrapped in pale green serrated leaves, a dream plant for a shrub bed or wild garden. John Codring-ton, another great gardener – and *not* mean, he is the most hospitable man in the world – gave me the seed years ago. It did not germinate for ages, then suddenly took off.

Many of the euphorbias have yellow-green flowers, of which the shrubby *E. polychroma* is the most striking, but I am also fond of the small, leafy *E. cyparissias* which runs about fairly harmlessly, of *E. robbiae*, with pale green flowers above dark green rosettes of leaves, and of *E. myrsinites*, which trails over a wall and seems to flower round the year.

The most perfect plant of all in this colour range is

Alchemilla mollis, of which you have plenty. I think that all lime-green flowers, if you cut them, look best mixed with white flowers, but I must warn you that the smyrnium wilts in a warm room. It likes to be really cold.

Aren't the primroses extraordinary this year? It must be two months since the first buds flowered and they are still at it. They have seeded in every bank, every crack in the paving, every tree stump. It is as though, chased from the woods, they were determined to re-establish their colonies in our gardens. Perhaps the cowslips will do the same – I was delighted to hear that you have seen quite a lot of them while riding on the downs, as I thought they had disappeared from our district.

May

Church Flowers

Dear Clare,

When I was on the church flower roster, from which I was granted a merciful release on the grounds of bad knees, one of my Sundays always came in early May, when the daffodils were over and the lilac had not opened, let alone the roses. Sometimes I bought flowers, an admission of defeat which was rightly despised by the village. 'How generous of you to spend so much on lilies' was not quite kindly meant.

My garden is in fact full of flowers in May, but they are wildish flowers which like cool, moist air around them and hate to be picked – pulmonarias, oxlips, forget-me-nots, smyrnium, doronicum, and so on. The abounding flowering shrubs, like the viburnums and deutzias, drop their petals when picked and scatter them on the floor, much to the annoyance of the kind ladies who sweep up. And the aubrietas and other rock plants are equally useless. The only good church flowers I had in May were the tulips and, dotted through the borders, it was a sacrifice to pick them. I had to say to myself, 'I am doing this for the Lord.'

So it is worth giving a thought to May purely from the cut-flower point of view, and I think that just three or four plantings would answer the church problem which you have inherited from me, and they would also be welcome, of course, for the house.

First, it's an idea to have just one small bed crammed with tulips solely for cutting – yellow and orange tulips show up well against the grey stone of the crusader tombs in the church. Then, the pale yellow peony 'Mlok', which I am always boring on about, flowers in early May, well before the double peonies, and will last a week in water. The late and lovely scented *poeticus* narcissi, such as Pheasant's Eye, should last well into May, especially if you hold them back by planting them in the shade. And the mixed pink, blue and white Spanish bluebells, *Scilla campanulata*, though stiff, look quite tolerable in vases softened with cow parsley, one of my favourite garden flowers, although anathema to the kind of man who mows the grass. John Codrington uses cow parsley to edge the winding walks in his romantic garden in Rutland. He told me it was scorned as a weed by crass garden visitors until he labelled it *Anthriscus sylvestris*, since when it has been much admired.

PS Since writing this, I have had a talk on the telephone with Barbara Moray, who was once as great a gardener as her daughter Arabella Boxer is a cook, and she told me she had lunched at the weekend with a friend who had a big bowl of *Cytisus praecox* on the table. It would never have occurred to me to cut this shrub, but you have a fine bush of it and it would look splendid in the church. Barbara said her friend is 'potty about gardening, she hasn't grown out of it yet', and I know how she feels. I seem to be full of misinformation about brooms, because I did not think your cytisus would do well on chalk. I am glad you ignored my Cassandra warnings.

Gardener's Question Time

Dear C,

I must say, the Gardener's-Question-Time-for-Charity business has become a major industry, as cut-throat as motorcars
or electronics. I am much in demand as a panel member for
these occasions not, I fear, for my advanced gardening
knowledge, but because my long experience on *My Word!*
with beloved Norden and Muir and Dilys gives me some
spurious authority.

But these amateur events are much more competitive than
a professional panel game, the rivalry being keen both
among the organisers to get the panel members they want,
and among the 'experts' themselves. I was rung up this week
by a grand lady in Hampshire asking me to join her panel
who was quite furious when she heard I had taken on,
months ago, another panel in the same district. Hardly my
fault.

And I have grown wary about my fellow panel members.
The atmosphere on *My Word!* was relaxed and friendly, we
enjoyed good answers whoever gave them, our common idea
being to achieve a successful entertainment, not to score
personal points. But amateur panel members strive to out-
smart each other. The rosy-cheeked, silver-haired lady
gardeners are the worst, they strive to shine, and are up to all
sorts of wheezes to grab the easy questions and palm off the
tough ones on suckers like me. Not my idea of a jolly
Saturday afternoon. Luckily, I tend now to forget the plant
names which once tripped so easily off my tongue, so I won't
be asked much longer.

Bedding Plants

Dear C,

We are now coming up to the (to me) dreaded season of
bedding plants. Not so dreaded by you, who still have a whiff
of the instant gardener about you. They should be planted
out now, or as soon as you think the frosts are over.

Bedding plants are essential to give the garden a lift in the
horrid month of August. By late July the first lot of border
plants has died an ugly death, the shrub and rambler roses are
a dreary tangle of brown flowers, even the honeysuckle and
alchemilla are spent. The hypericums and day lilies do their
best, but it is not enough. One must try to fill the gaps,
especially in the borders.

Great border gardeners, like Christopher Lloyd, grow
hundreds of bedding plants for late summer when their
borders are at their best, but use only choice and sometimes
little-known varieties. The over-quoted Miss Jekyll would
sink bedding plants in the borders *in pots* to ensure a constant
succession of well-modulated groups of flowers, which seems
to me gross cheating.

Neither you nor I can raise our own plants in our present
circumstances – I did it in a modest way when Percy came in
from the village to water the greenhouse every evening, a
man of few words, but what a treasure – so we are more or
less confined to the limited ranges in the garden centres. I
can make only a few skimpy suggestions as to choice and
management, this being a subject on which I am for once
reluctant to pontificate.

When you buy, choose plants in an early stage of develop-
ment. Little plants will transfer better from box to garden,
and of course will have more of a future life – it's not a lot of
use if the bedding plants finish along with the early perennials. Don't buy too many, for they will need constant
watering if the summer is dry, their roots being shallow. You
could ask Phyllis to water a few chosen spots for you in

mid-week, but she couldn't water all over the garden, you know how busy she is.

I think that only a few kinds look well in wildish gardens like yours and mine. Tobacco plant, with its wayward style, looks right almost anywhere and flowers for months, and the white ones smell heavenly. Ivy-leaved geraniums and scented-leaved geraniums are also long-lasting and fit in better than the grander but stiffer regal and zonal pelargoniums, which look their best in pots. (Geraniums in huge variety, many with beautiful leaves and spicy scents, can be bought by mail order.) Heliotrope is a nice old-fashioned plant with a lovely scent, but a bit sombre in colour.

I also have a weakness for some of the plants my mother used to grow in our small London garden, especially snapdragons, petunias and canterbury bells, but you may not agree. Snapdragons flower from midsummer right into autumn, so do petunias in sunny weather, but canterbury bells have a short season and leave you with spaces to fill in for the second time. When I was a child, men used to tour the London streets with barrows of plants, we always bought some, and very good they were. There were also magnificent pansies, another reliable bedder, but you must deadhead almost every day.

How do you feel about dahlias? They look absolutely wrong in my garden. I have tried them everywhere and they are not good mixers, and they need a lot of feeding, watering and staking, not to mention being plagued by earwigs, which you are supposed to trap in disgusting ways. But dahlias are bliss for cutting, large, showy, vulgar, and good for the ego – it seems clever to have grown anything so large. All these plants need full sun, but you have plenty.

Of course, good gardeners have forests of late perennials as well as bedding plants in August, but I never seem to have enough, perhaps because I do not care for the yellow and orange daisy perennials which are August staples. But I will go over to Esther Merton's later this year, clutching my notebook in my hand, to get ideas. Her borders are celebrated and were a triumph on television, Esther and Roy Lancaster carrying on a spirited crosstalk act.

Although I buy my summer bedding plants at garden centres, where professionals have done the nursery work, I want to make a little patch of fine raked soil in the next three or four weeks to sow a packet of my favourite spring bedding plants, wall-flowers, which I love for their soft colours and cottagey scent. When the seedlings are of appreciable size, they should be lifted and planted out about 9 inches apart, to allow plenty of room for strong roots to grow. They will be finally transplanted in October to that narrow bed in the sunk garden which is protected by a wall. Unfortunately, wallflowers only do well with me in a mild winter, and I have often lost them to violent winds or frosts, but they are worth the risk.

Spoiled Buds

Oh, darling, I think you were amazingly stoical, I wanted to cry. Your wisteria buds are dropping off and it is largely my fault. There is not a trace of pest or disease and the only reason I can think of is lack of water.. In dry weather like this, one waters the smaller, more vulnerable plants and forgets the trees and shrubs, and I suppose your wisteria, though several years old, is not yet sufficiently established to forage for itself. I ought to have noticed, I feel terrible about it. You said the buds were not developing properly and I gave you false reassurance.

The only hope I can offer, and it is a faint one, is that there may be a few flowers later on and that the buckets of water you have now applied will fill out the buds. Just one lovely drooping tassel would lighten my guilt. Please forgive.

Birdsong

Dear C,

Osbert used to get very cross when he was woken at 5 a.m. by the dawn chorus. 'Why must they kick up a row in the middle of the night?' As he loved birds, and had a pair of field-glasses which he never managed to focus (and what glasses could out-see those huge, bulging blue eyes?), this was most unreasonable of him.

Tragically, there is no dawn chorus any more and scarcely any bird song at any time, owing to the disgusting magpies which prey on the eggs and chicks of the songbirds. I have consulted farming friends and find that it is almost impossible to destroy the horrible creatures. They are difficult to shoot. The only effective method is to poison them, which is illegal, and though I might not mind a bit of lawbreaking if it would tempt back the wrens, nut-hatches, tree-creepers, tits, warblers and wagtails which used to dart about the place, I do not know how to do it. The poison is dangerous and has to be carefully put in place.

The only songbirds which seem able to resist the predators are blackbirds, and the garden is still full of the brave creatures, the first to sing in the morning and the last to sing at night. I suppose they are strong enough to fight off the enemy. There are also a few blue-tits about, but I tremble for them, and for a wren which I think has nested in the pile of brushwood near the rubbish heap.

Birds are as important to me in the garden as plants, and I hope that nature will rouse herself and look into the magpie problem, though I don't feel optimistic. There are no proper gamekeepers any more, only Thatcher-type 'managers' of the local shoots, and as the pheasants are now reared in pens like poultry, where the magpies cannot get at them, it is in nobody's interest to strike the wretches down.

One ray of hope . . . I think that Nick's new devotion to target practice with an air rifle may be beginning to scare the magpies a bit. I have a faint feeling that they have diminished in numbers in the last few weeks. But how to explain to the songbirds that those bangs are not aimed at them?

I wish I were musical enough to distinguish the varied songs of birds. I cannot go far beyond nightingales, blackbirds, larks, thrushes and owls, and cannot possibly identify the twitterings of all the warblers. I hear there is a pianist, a retired Professor of Music, who has made a study of birdsong, recording their tunes, slowing up the tapes (for birds sing at tremendous speed), transcribing the notes into manuscript and then playing them on the piano. He compares the tunes with some of the themes of Beethoven.

Bright Colours

Dear C,

My trip to Jordan has whetted my appetite for colour. Just as children like bright toys and picture-books, so does the budding gardener tend to aim for a garish garden, graduating as time goes on to softer, subtler colours. By the time he is middle-aged and connoisseurish, a gardener may be growing nothing but greenish-greyish-whiteish flowers, grasses and foliage plants. He is encouraged in this by a bevy of good-taste gardening books. I never belonged to the ultra-discreet school myself, but neither do I enjoy a bed of salmon-pink roses edged with double marigolds.

In the Jordan climate, where summer comes suddenly, like a thunderclap, all the spring flowers come out at once, and blue geraniums, crimson poppies, orange marigolds and inky gladioli make a carpet of unrestrained brilliance. This is wholly appropriate where the sun blazes from blue skies, but can such vivid colours blend with our watercolour landscape? I think the answer may be that many hybrid flowers (which are often too large as well as too bright) look uneasy in an English setting, while a species looks at home even if it comes from far across the world. By species I mean a plant in its wild form, or something very near it, a cross which preserves the plant's true nature.

Of the brilliant species which look quite natural in my garden, my favourite is the crown imperial fritillary, and I feel great pride in my orange and yellow clumps. The crown imperial comes from Persia and the Himalaya, so it might well look pretentious among the forget-me-nots and polyanthus sitting humbly at its feet but, being a species, it never looks amiss. Occasionally crown imperials come up blind, and some experts tell you to plant the bulbs on their sides to keep the rain out of their hollow centres, but I think a better answer is to give them masses of manure. Would you like to try them?

Another theatrical flower which adapts well to the English scene is the tiger lily, *L. tigrinum*, which I once saw growing wild in Japan, on an otherwise disastrous trip for the *Daily Express*. This is not for you or me, for the tiger lily hates lime, but in gardens which suit it this spotted orange lily does not look an intruder. Another bright flower which I love and can grow is one of the shrubby euphorbias, *E. polychroma*, with sulphur-yellow flowers. Again, it's a species. So is the *Fuchsia magellicana* which is used for cottage hedges all over Cornwall, although it comes from Mexico and Peru, while the hybrid fuchsias look foolish in England except as pot plants.

I don't want to labour this point about species to absurdity because many flowers have been 'improved' with taste and restraint, often with the advantage that the hybrid blooms for a longer period than the species. But when a flower of gaudy colour looks just right in England, it is usually a wild flower from somewhere. Perhaps Jordan.

Magic Powers

Dear Clare,

That brush-cutter which Nick bought on Saturday is the most sublime invention since the electric blanket. I swear to you by every oath honoured by gardeners that I did not ask him to cut my rough grass, let alone trim the whiskers along my grass paths, nor even hint at such a thing, and if he whizzed through my garden before yours it must have been because my grass was longer and more of a challenge.

It is a truly magical machine. If I bought one for myself, could I learn to use it or would I cut my leg off? Please advise.

Dear M,

The chief disadvantage to the brush-cutter is the fashion accessory that goes with it. You have to don large and exceedingly unflattering plastic goggles which steam up very quickly and don't enhance either the hair or the face. Vanity aside, it does require a certain amount of nerve, and if used for any length of time becomes rather heavy. I believe you can buy a strap for it, which Nicks plans to send for. I did notice him leaning slightly to the left after prolonged use last weekend.

It is great fun to use. It reaches areas where no man has gone before, and with the speed of light. It comes with a nylon cord for cutting weak growth, or an alarming serrated metal blade for hewing down suckers. It is easy to get carried away with the excitement. Nick has removed several plants just when they were beginning to naturalise nicely down the banks, but you can't have everything. It is also very noisy. I think if we both had one the neighbours might rampage.

I could lend you Nick from time to time on a temporary basis. He will get frustrated unless he gets enough space to whir about in, and it will save on two lots of hospital bills.

Chelsea Splendour

Dear Clare,

Carnivores and epiphytes, tropical pools and alpine land-
scapes, spires of lupins, arcades of roses, cohorts of fuchsias
in purple and gold, mountains of vegetables, giant begonias
glaring at dwarf bonsai – I and my colleagues on the judging
committees agreed that this was the most splendiferous
Chelsea Flower Show we have ever seen. None was so blasé
as to disagree. In the artificial conditions of a show one
applauds plants which are so strange, even barbaric, that
they would have no meaning for one in normal life, but the
sheer panache with which they are grown and displayed
inspires admiration and awe. It is like getting involved at the
theatre with the tribulations of King Lear, who would seem
just a tiresome old gentleman if one met him socially.

I think the rare intensity of light we have experienced
through this hot, dry May has much to do with the extra
depth of colour in many of the flowers. In the over-eighties
heat today, some of the plants are already wilting, and I fear
the show must flag as the week goes on, but for the fortunate
early birds it has been a brilliant experience. My tired feet
are like pig's trotters, legs running straight into feet without
any ankles between, not pretty, but it has been worth it. I
walked round every inch of the show in the morning and
judged in my section in the afternoon, with a jolly lunch in
between, *bien placée* between Maurice Mason and Lord
Aberconway, so I have had a busy day.

If the marquee was gorgeous, the outdoor gardens were
more to my taste than usual. Sometimes they offer more for
the monumental mason than the plantsman, with massed
rhodos set in sheets of paving or elaborate brickwork, but
this year they are less pretentious. I wish you could see the
Alpine Garden Society's exhibit planted with more than two
thousand different rock plants looking fresh and natural
among trickling waterfalls. And I think you might get

hooked on the idea of a conservatory, a Georgian and Victorian fashion resurgent in the 1980s. If you fancy one for your south wall, I warn you there might be a gap between appearance and reality, for conservatories are not an easy path to gracious living. Too often there are red spiders in the canapés and whitefly in the champagne.

Britain can certainly put on a flower show better than any other country in the world – it is the variety of plants which is unique. Darling, I would have loved to buy you a ticket for tomorrow, and I have to go back myself, but you say you are booked with jobs for every hour this week. Needless to say, Max is going to the £75-gala this evening, but even that is in the way of business, as the *Telegraph* has a garden at the show. How hard my children work.

The Invaders

Dearest C,

At this season of explosive growth, some of my gardening mistakes are painfully obtrusive. I cannot ignore the greedy, land-hungry plants which I was foolish enough to invite into the garden years ago. Be warned.

The plant invaders attack you with guile. They have smiling faces. They offer to share your property on friendly terms. They promise to help you keep it furnished and tidy. Then they show their true nature and swamp everything else, the cuckoos of the plant world. Some of my invaders arrived of their own accord and I failed to control them, but others I planted as 'ground cover', a term which must be regarded with the gravest suspicion. This weekend, I have been morbidly counting the fruits of my follies.

The worst invaders are plants which spread by layering (they send out arching shoots which root wherever they touch the ground); they increase at express speed and are almost ineradicable. Beware, particularly, of periwinkles and the native archangel, or *Lamiastrum galeobdolon*. Some of my periwinkles were here when I started but I positively introduced the *Vinca difformis* which is such a nuisance in the front beds under the house, being very untidy and able to climb – it persecutes the roses and it roots very deep. I was enticed by its white winter flowers, the summer flowers being the usual periwinkle blue. I was once troubled with the all-smothering white *Cerastium tomentosum*, or snow-in-summer, which sneaked in of its own accord, but I did get rid of it eventually.

These are all fairly obviously weeds, but some choicer flowers can cause permanent trouble. I would be wary of bluebells. If allowed, they will colonise large areas and seed all over the place, and the bulbs go deep and are difficult to dig up. Another pernicious bulb is the grape hyacinth. The herbaceous yellow pimpernel, *Lysimachia punctata*, is a charming plant for the wild garden, but is too greedy for a mixed border. Japanese anemones are hard to control, while the lovely alstroemerias, or Peruvian lilies, creep about and shoot up incongruously in the middle of shrubs, rose bushes and herbaceous clumps of poppies or delphiniums. In fact, alstroemerias look so unreal that I think they are best grown in a bed of their own. Surprisingly, they are perfectly hardy and are good cutting flowers.

I think you have no invited invaders so far, only the weeds we are bound to have living in the heart of open country where every breeze is laden with seeds. Don't weaken and let the intruders in.

Dear M,

You have possibly sent out a warning in the nick of time although, in spite of your parental guidelines, I am tempted to slot in a few bluebells down by the woodland wild garden. Is this very wayward? One of the ravishing sights of the year is a walk through our woods when the bluebells are in flower. A sea of lilac colour dappled by sun through the beech leaves gives even this old cynic a lift for the day. I do realise my patch is smaller in scale, but perhaps just a few?

I am also dead set on getting that very steep bank covered with something, the one which leads down to the car layby. The brush-cutter has triumphed over the nettles, and now the site looks distinctly naked. It is much too steep for a mixed planting, a goodly invader may be just the answer. What did you say that periwinkle was called?

Magpie Saga
(*continued*)

Dear Clare,

Congratulate Nick from me, he is a worthy successor to my friends the poachers and trappers of yore. Yesterday he shot a rabbit on my lawn, today he put out the corpse as bait and shot a magpie. I am becoming as bloodthirsty as your father and brother. The other evening I watched a thrush singing his heart out on the top of the tallest and most ancient apple tree, a song I have not heard for the last three years. The battle is being won.

Nick was rash enough to show me a Victorian book for shooting men which recommended the following method for despatching magpies. 'Put on a lady's cloak and bonnet, keep the gun by your side with the muzzle down under the cloak, and then walk towards the bird in a circular direction with the eyes turned another way; the bird will allow the sportsman so dressed to get within shot.' I greeted this with enthusiasm, but apart from the difficulty of finding a becoming bonnet, Nick is reluctant to be seen in the village in drag.

June

Deadheading

Dear Child,

I'm afraid you are always going to feel a pang of disappointment when you get to your cottage on Friday evenings. It is the weekender's fate to find that in his brief absence the garden has gone to pot. Your instinct is to rush for the mower and bash the grass until nightfall, but I suggest a quieter evening – get the secateurs and deadhead. It is dead blooms, especially on the roses, which make a garden look flowerless and neglected. Half an hour spent deadheading would make it look young and fresh again and full of buds.

The deadheading season starts in earnest with the larger bulbs. We all know that daffodil leaves must be left until they shrivel to feed the bulbs, but if you cut off the dead *flowers* the plants will look quite tidy. Similarly, deadhead the crown imperials and the tulips – one tatty tulip in a group of a dozen pulls down the whole effect. Later in the season, deadhead the peonies and delphiniums and other herbaceous things religiously, unless of course you want to keep a few flowerheads for seed.

Rock plants, like helianthemums and *Iberis sempervirens*, and spring ground-cover plants, like doronicum and pulmonaria, have too many flowers to cut singly, so shear them over when brown and faded, and you will soon get mounds of fresh leaves and perhaps a few more flowers.

A bigger problem is that of rambler roses, which present a dismal sight when the first grand flowering has gone sour. No hope of deadheading completely. But the job is easier if you choose low-growing ramblers rather than the giants, or roses which shed their dead flowers instead of clinging to the corpses. That is why I prefer The New Dawn to Albertine for the front of the cottage.

Shrub roses and floribundas also look much fresher after dead-heading, and if you make it a proper pruning job, the bushes will benefit. So instead of snipping off dead flowers, trim away the whole faded shoot, cutting back to just above a young shoot. It takes no longer, and the young shoot will grow on and give you more flowers later on. This is true of nearly all roses except some of the old-fashioned ones which flower only once.

If you deadhead on Friday evening you will wake on Saturday to a garden reborn, and Nick, exulting in his new machinery, might opt to cut the grass while you and Calypso go cantering over the horizon.

By the way, do keep Calypso short of cash this month and next. I need help in raking up my deadheads and would pay top rates if she would rally.

Random Design

Dear C,

Half-way mark in the year, and I have been thinking about the design of your garden, which is different from mine and, in fact, fits in better with the site. Both gardens slope in two directions, north to south and east to west, so that symmetry is almost impossible to achieve; if the slope were in one direction only, one could terrace it.

Many years ago, when my garden was smaller, I made the central path leading to the statue of Actaeon under the arch of roses and honeysuckle. The vista is a success and the borders either side of the path have their moments, especially in spring; but later they develop at different speeds, owing to the variety of light, moisture, and so on, so that the effect is lopsided. As I extended the garden, I made island beds or planted banks wherever they happened to be, and the effect is more natural and altogether more attractive.

By luck or flair, you have made no attempt at symmetry anywhere. Your garden consists of separate small trees or large shrubs, each in a bed with underplanting. Your Bramley apple tree has forget-me-nots and hellebores, your dry bank has broom and viburnum with alchemilla, hardy geraniums and a few bedding plants. Your bit of copse, where the trees are closer and the ground is shady, has primroses, foxgloves, and so on. This very simple idea is wonderfully workable and the curved beds have the advantage that they can be extended at any time to make room for more plants.

If I started again, I would do something like it. No straight walks, but everything gently curved, perhaps gates in the boundary hedges carrying the eye to the marvellous views of the downs beyond. My instinct is always to enclose myself, like a hibernating animal, and I have a secret fear of a theme park on the downs, with neolithic mock-ups wrecking the skyline. But even so, a more outward-looking garden on a freer plan might have been more appropriate for the site.

A Pot Garden

Dear Clare,

One day last year I looked out of the bathroom window in
your London flat on to a boring square of roof about the size
of a kitchen. A month or two later the bathroom had grown
a french window and I walked out into a flowery outdoor
room complete with barbecue. Roses climbed up the wall of
the house, clematis twined round the encircling balustrade,
it was a transformation scene. Having no gift myself for roof
or balcony gardening – I am only at ease working in open soil
– I am wondering if you could bear to record (so that I can
pinch your ideas in future) how on earth you did it?

Dear M,

When you are a flat-dweller, any area of outdoor space is a
major bonus. I first became inspired on a hot, sunny day
walking to the postbox. I noticed a couple barbecueing on
their balcony and, not to be outdone, I rushed to the local
garage, purchased my own barbecue and charcoal and
proceeded to gain access to a very small area of roof outside
the bathroom. At first this was not easy and required some
mountaineering skills. Friends were made to clamber into
the bath and then squeeze through a gap in the window (the
sash cord had broken), and once outside nobody dared to
move owing to lack of safety harness and railings. Now it's all
very chic. I've moved the bath, you can shimmy through
french doors, cling to the barley-sugar twisted railings and
peer at the privileged in the gardens below.

Roof gardening is one of life's great pleasures, and is not
referred to as container gardening for nothing. Everything is
manageable, deadheading is a doddle, weeding non-existent,
and you can re-organise colour schemes by shifting the pots
around. The disadvantages are removing the débris, heaving

bags of peat up several flights, ceaseless watering and, if you are very unlucky and misjudge the weight, house subsidence.

I was very fortunate when I started planning because I went on a business trip to Spain. The unlucky van driver was commissioned on his homeward journey to stop off and fill the truck with terracotta pots. He took the task seriously, which was an excellent beginning. The English garden centres stock pots which are either cheap and dull or very pricey.

I wasn't creative at the start. Geraniums and fuchsias, the staples of the window-box, were potted everywhere. Now the whole effect is more haphazard and rambling. You *must* cram the pots. I try to fill every space, however small, with something. My pride and joy is the rose The New Dawn that is halfway up the wall now. I count the buds each week (you can do this with terrace gardening) and spray madly for greenfly. A clematis, C. Jackmanii, shares the same tub, along with some ivy and, this year, alyssum, pansies and violas. I am fond of my pot of alchemilla, it reminds me of the cottage and stands next to a tub of African daisies which have come through the winter. A lot of plants that are supposedly annual have managed to survive the frosts and are carrying on blooming, which is rather pleasing; my roof is obviously very sheltered.

Last year I grew sweet peas in a trough, which were a great success and looked very pretty twisted through the railings. I wish I had room to grow a row of beans or courgettes, perhaps I could just fit in another box – I rather fancy the idea of 'beans Finborough Road'.

I don't know why you think you have no gift for roof gardening. There is nothing to do. I feed all the plants with liquid tomato fertilizer from time to time, water prodigiously each evening, otherwise you plan as the season goes along, transforming boxes in the time it takes you to go to the garden centre and back.

I do long to expand. Did you know that my main roof is flat? I am desperate to bang a hole up to it, and then I can start fully indulging my pot fantasies.

My Balcony

Dear Clare,

Your letter about Pot Gardening is inspirational. Could I, should I, do something about my naked balcony in London? And would you come with an initial batch of pots, peat and plants?

A Dry Bank

Dear Clare,

Already the besetting sin of your garden and mine – dryness of soil – is revealing itself after a month of minimal rain following a dry winter, and a few shrubs are flagging. You asked me some time ago to suggest shrubs for your dry bank, and I have been thinking about those which have withstood drought well in my own patches of Arizona.

I am afraid some of them are rather boring, and I would not now plant buddleias, berberis or potentillas. But I have had much pleasure from philadelphus, especially *P. Beau-clerk* (huge white flowers with a swoony scent), *Viburnum burkwoodii* (tennis balls of pink scented flowers in April and nice shiny leaves), hypericums (St John's Wort flowers in July and August) and, above all, from Mediterranean sub-shrubs, such as *Phlomis fruticosa* (Jerusalem Sage) and common rosemary. These are mostly wild plants of the maquis, of which Osbert and I would crush and sniff the leaves on our aromatic walks in Corsica – you were too young at that time to appreciate the plants, being more interested in the young waiter with the curly hair: that was a saga. But though drought-resistant, they are not very hardy in England; this is particularly true of the papery cistuses and starry myrtle which grew in the Corsican hinterland behind the quiet sunny beaches. I have grown these at home and pulled them through mild winters, but they succumb to a harsh one, as does the Tuscan rosemary, which has flowers of an exceptionally deep blue. Needing special care, these not-quite-hardy shrubs invite the special affection so often given to a delicate child.

Returning to your dry bank, your *Cytisus praecox* is a triumph, a fountain of pale gold in May, and you might like to try another broom, the dwarfer *Genista lydia* which sprays about in the same graceful manner. On the other hand, I am nervous about your *Viburnum plicatum* Mariesii, which ought to be established after two or three years, but seems to need buckets of water in every dry spell. I would be inclined to move it in the autumn to a damper spot. My own deutzias also tend to wilt in prolonged dry weather, and the cornuses are thirsty plants – I am afraid my showpiece *Cornus controversa* Variegata may be going home.

One shrub which I have not grown, but I can't think why, is the elder with finely cut golden leaves called *Sambucus racemosa* Plumosa Aurea. It likes dry soil, though Beth Chatto says it needs shade from the hottest sun. Not, perhaps, for your sunny bank, but you have several wild elders in your copse, and might replace one of them with this smart relation. It is quite sensational, with brilliant yellow leaves in spring which turn to lemon yellow later on.

Of course, there are lots of herbaceous plants for dry places, mostly of a daisy nature with yellow or tawny flowers in August; we might think about them when the time comes. But your bank is already well planted at the base, it is only the dry summit which needs bolstering with something a bit choice. You might shortlist *Philadelphus* Beauclerk, *Hypericum inodorum* Elstead (smaller flowers than *H.* Hidcote, but bright red berries appear simultaneously), *Phlomis fruticosa*, more brooms, and, taking a frost risk, the orchid pink *Cistus purpureus*.

The Scent of Flowers

Dear Clare,

We all know about Proust's madeleines, and how taste remembered inspired twelve volumes of recollections. But to Proust scent was equally evocative. 'We would be met on our way by the scent of his [Swann's] lilac trees, come out to welcome strangers.' 'Often I have wished to see a person again without realising that it was simply because that person recalled to me a hedge of hawthorns in blossom.'

Scent as a spur to memory means much more to most of us than taste – the only taste which lingers on my tongue is that of a fresh-baked lobster pizza shared with a dear friend on Capri, and lobster pizza is too rare an experience with me to loom large.

To me herbs have the most beautiful scent of all, and I shall never forget the scent of the mountains at Tolon, in Greece. The old house we rented one summer (long ago pulled down) had a back door which opened straight on to the mountain behind, and I would walk out every day to pick thyme and marjoram for omelettes – eggs then were about the only food which was plentiful, with an occasional lamb chop. The whole countryside was impregnated with the scent of herbs, which in my English garden seem to smell of nothing at all. They need great heat.

Lilac reminds me of walks in London with my mother, for lilac was then the common shrub in every London garden. Gardenias remind me of that beauty of the twenties, Edwina d'Erlanger, who used the same gardenia scent all her life. (Women shouldn't keep changing the scent they use, the right one becomes part of their personality.) Primrose scent takes me back to those quiet Berkshire holidays with my brother, when I used to pick bunches of them, pack them in damp moss, and post them home. Azaleas recall the Moat Walk at Sissinghurst, where I spent delectable days working on my book. Leaf-mould reminds me of Tennyson's perverse reaction to that delicious smell. 'My very heart faints and my whole soul grieves/At the moist rich smell of the rotting leaves.' White jasmine never smelled sweeter than at John Betjeman's cottage in Cornwall, where the flow of conversation between John and Osbert ranged from the indignant to the hilarious. 'I say, old top, have you heard what they're doing to the choir-stalls at St Hamburger's-by-the-Sewer?' and so on. Mrs Sinkin pinks were the glory of the White Border at Glyndebourne before the war, their rich scent blending with the background noises of the orchestra tuning up. They are not widely grown today, for their season is brief and specialists complain that their calyxes split, as if one cared. Give me one Mrs Sinkin with her calyx split rather than a bunch of pink Doris, their calyces entire.

Do have lots of scented plants in your garden, especially those with which you have happy associations, for memory enhances life, particularly in solitude.

Magpie Saga
(continued)

Dear Clare,

I am becoming a Little Englander. Brave little Britain must stand alone. The EC in Brussels is proposing that the magpie should be made a protected bird. This can only have been thought up by the French, who slaughter all their small birds in what is ludicrously called *la chasse*, so that there are no magpies. No prey, no predator. This ill-conceived regulation must be fought beak and claw.

Beautiful Rough Grass

Dear Clare,

We both tend to be martyrs to our grass, trying to make lawns on rough, dry, chalky slopes. Yesterday I saw a lovely garden which is quite shaggy, a garden which I had written about fifteen years ago, when it was nothing but a field and the planting was all in the mind, Roy Strong's garden in Herefordshire. Today it is a dream of green, the many greens of trees, of hedges and topiary, of long meadow grass and grassy walks, some straight, some meandering, but each one leading to some charming piece of statuary – a pinnacle from All Souls or a little Victorian temple with (appropriately for Roy) period busts of Victoria and Albert. It is a relaxed and happy garden, hedges sprouting wildly, hairy topiary shrubs patiently waiting their turn for the clippers, long grass not cut until the end of July, paths mown once a fortnight. Not a herbaceous border anywhere, the whole garden is non-Jekyll. Roy and Julia and I wandered down the long alleys and through the hedged enclosures and down the pleached lime walk for two hours while I gulped in the greenness and freshness.

'I have been so happy making it,' Roy said, 'it is three and a half acres of private world. I can take long walks in it, I can read in it, I can clip my bushes in it all day long. I take out the radio and turn on Radio 4 – it's mostly ethnic plays or about Ireland – but I am as happy as a sandboy; I was once listening too closely and I cut off the head of a box pyramid, but it didn't bother me. I like all the roughness, the grass which is grass, not lawn. I like my garden shabby at the edges, I can leave it without disaster. And I love shaping the topiary, the pyramids and pompoms and rusticated columns. There are dozens of bushes to be clipped. I start in May and work round until all are done.'

Roy says that the garden has not cost a lot of money. 'The All Souls pinnacles were crumbling and going cheap. Most of the statues are reproductions, they soon acquire lichen; and the few old ones I picked up here and there. I now badly want a statue of Flora, but that is to be positively the last or the garden will look like a churchyard. Another thing, all the trees and hedging plants were bought very small at minimum prices, and, as well as being cheaper, small plants grow more quckly than large ones. Those yew arches started as 18-inch sprigs, and the eucalyptus tree was given to me in a yogurt container by a friend.

'Nor do I have a lot of professional help: I have two local boys who each give us a day a fortnight, one devotes a whole day to mowing in the growing season. They are marvellous; they are probably making patios for bungalows the rest of the time, but as soon as they come here they enter into the classical spirit. The rest we do ourselves. The woodland garden is Julia's, full of hellebores and pulmonaria and cowslips, and Julia does the rose garden – shrub roses only – and the vegetable garden and the compost heaps, and the two orchards are hers. The small one has thirty ornamental apple trees, the large one about sixty different edible apples, including some old historic varieties.'

Though the garden is wildish, it is far from random; there is a firm structure of enclosures and walks. Roy planned it on paper fifteen years ago, and the plan has changed very little. The inspiration is seventeenth century 'with vistas like the Kip engravings'. The topiary is, I suppose, of Dutch origin. The plants which are clipped are not only box, yew and cypress, but hawthorn, amelanchier, euonymus, all sorts of surprises.

As well as green, there is much white in the garden, white roses, white narcissus in the long grass, and white wild flowers, with lots of cow parsley. And in winter there is brown, especially the caramel brown of the beech hedges, which retain their leaves.

This is not a scheme which would suit your garden or mine in the slightest degree, and the soil is sandy, of which we haven't a grain. What impresses, and makes me aware that I try too hard, is the lack of struggle, the shagginess which is not untidiness, but freedom.

Dear M,

You keep mentioning friends who inspire you and invite you to share their gardens. So as not to be outdone I will tell you about two of mine. Both have cottage gardens bulging with so many ideas that when I return to mine I set to with new gusto and determination to do better.

You have met nearly all my friends, but as yet you have still to be introduced to James Wedge. In the week he photographs languid models for magazines, but at the weekend he hides himself away in the centre of the Forest of Dean with his wife Amanda, and creates the ultimate in cottage gardens.

In James's country world, the garden and the landscape become one. The end of the garden drops away to give a breathtaking view of fields and forest right over to Gloucester twinkling away on the horizon. When he first bought the cottage, like me, he knew nothing about gardening but, unlike me, he read about it. Every bed is planted and then over-planted. All his flowers and vegetables are grown from seed and the beds are filled to bursting with cottage plants. His garden is everything I would like mine to be, waving hollyhocks and delphiniums, clematis and honeysuckle and rustic poles. It is a romantic garden nurtured with great love. James spends all day in the garden from first to last light. If he isn't digging, he will be off collecting tree bark from the forest, or organising the extensive vegetable garden. Amanda is a gardening widow who says she is going blind from pricking out the seed trays. I find the ambience truly magical, and if you are very good I will see if I can wangle you an invitation to visit.

The other garden is dug by someone you know very well, one of my oldest friends, film director Steve Campbell, who lives in a converted chapel. Steve's ideas are not constrained in any way by the pocket size of the garden. The first project was to build a pond, well more of a lake really – it certainly takes up half the space, and is filled with rushes and reeds and lilies. I'm afraid the fish have been eaten by a local heron keen on a choice feast. The garden also boasts a minute orchard (heaven help the trees when they mature), a rustic walk through the wild area, past the roses, a sundial and a large stone dog. Steve is mad for you to pay another visit, he has a great number of questions for you. He much admires your span of *Viburnum* Mariesii and would construct a viburnum bank by the rose walk given an ounce of encouragement.

Watering

Dear C,

Our gardens look very thirsty, with cracks in the hard, dry soil, and we will have to water, an act of charity which turns us all into reluctant clowns, for no contraption is more mischievous than a hose. Mine wriggles like a serpent, explodes in my face, leaks at the joints, and stops just ten feet short of the young trees which need it most. And just when I am getting into my stride, the water pressure drops.

But water we must, and if we want to help the plants, we must water efficiently. This means watering in the cool of evening, after dark if necessary, so that the water will not instantly evaporate, and when the plants' pores are open and able to take the water in. Also, one must select the more vulnerable plants and water them thoroughly, rather than giving the garden an overall splash.

You know that my scientific knowledge is dismal but I can read, and I was recently impressed by an article in a Sunday magazine giving some startling facts. An actively growing lawn loses nine pints of water per square yard in a day. A tomato plant needs a third of a pint to produce one new leaf. Modern gardening favours crowded planting, which puts an abnormal strain on the supply of water in the soil. So when you water, see that the water goes deep down below the roots – a light sprinkling brings the roots up and does more harm than good. A can for each shrub two or three times a week is none too much, and give frequent soakings to seedlings and bedding plants.

Try not to water so violently that the earth cakes round the plants, for this will keep out the blessed rain when it comes at last. If the soil does cake, I usually prick it over with a fork to make it more porous. And if you don't object to a water-butt near the house, with a pipe to carry rain water from the roof-guttering into the butt, you will have some nice soft water instead of our horrible tap water, which is packed with lime and poisoned with chemicals galore. You know how quickly the kettles fur up with chalk, and I swear I can taste the nitrogen fertilizer which is showered on to the fields for wheat, more wheat, and still more wheat, mixed farming being a dying art on the Berkshire downs.

Real gardeners love rain (within limits), and I remember Mrs Margery Fish of honoured memory telling me that it made her feel positively ill to hear rain-water gurgling down a grating. She had water-butts by every garden building to store the rain, and enjoyed the sight and sound of them filling up.

I used to favour the old beer casks which were sold as water-butts as being more homely-looking than the modern plastic ones, but in spite of scrubbing they smelt strongly of beer and seemed to collect an unacceptable quantity of algae, insects and general muck.

How much of the present early drought following a dry winter is due to the 'greenhouse' effect I do not know. Of course I believe in the menace of a warming world and am appalled at the felling of forests and the pollution we create. But this mild winter followed two bitter ones, and the last two summers were cold and wet, so I think any conclusion that the English climate is warming fast is based on too little evidence. I would like less propaganda and harder facts.

Hardy Geraniums

Dearest Clare,

I don't seem to have written much lately about plants, and I would like to sing a little hymn in praise of hardy geraniums, or cranesbills, which are now in their prime. Yours are looking luscious, but might I suggest some more, for they are a huge family of about four hundred species, many of them hardy in this country, paragons of virtue, indeed they are hard to fault. They will grow in any soil, in sun or part-shade, and spread quickly into large leafy mounds. They make perfect ground cover, not empire building, but keeping their place, and fill in between roses, shrubs, or taller herbaceous plants without trying to outshine them or crawl all over them. If the clumps get too large, they are easily pulled up.

The flowers and leaves of geraniums are equally appealing; it is a great family for leaves, some of them toothed and deeply cut, some round-lobed. You already have the silvery pink *Geranium endressii*, which flowers all summer long, at the foot of your white Blanc Double de Coubert rugosa rose, and you have G. *macrorrhizum*, with pink flowers and aromatic leaves, which turn scarlet in autumn, by your front door. But you must find a place for Johnson's Blue, which is a little taller than the other two and produces a continuous stream of flowers from May until at least mid-July. If you shear over the plants after flowering, you will get new leaves almost between one weekend and the next, and probably a few more flowers later. These are very like the wild meadow cranesbill which is now making shimmering blue ribbons along the verges of the roads, but the wild plants flower for a much shorter season than Johnson's Blue, which is a hybrid.

You might also like to try an exciting geranium called G. *phaeum*, or Mourning Widow, the flowers being such a dark purple as to be almost black. I have always meant to grow it, but have never got round to it.

I do have two dwarf species which Hugh Johnson gave me from his garden in Essex, G. *renardii*, with palest lavender flowers veined with violet and velvety scalloped leaves, and G. *cinereum*, with tiny magenta flowers with black centres. Neither increases much, they are really rock plants, but I can give you bits if you want them.

I also have a taller hardy geranium which is not so much a ground-cover plant as a border plant in its own right, G. *psilostemon*, also with black-eyed magenta flowers, but more than an inch across. I could give you seedlings, they pop up all over the place. This was formerly called G. *armenum*, which seems sensible as its native home is Armenia, poor troubled land of wars and earthquakes, but the nomenclature boys have given it this clumsy new name.

This is malicious of me, but I might mention that your un-favourite Herb Robert, a pretty little weed which I am fond of, is a hardy geranium, the plant you nurtured for so long in a pot under the impression that it was a seedling of a tree peony. When it revealed its identity after two years of cosseting by producing some little pink flowers I heard you swear heartily, a rare occurrence, both of us having used impeccable language since Calypso became of listening and repeating age. 'Bloody hell,' you kept saying, 'bloody hell', with real anger. I laughed heartlessly, because as gardening tragedies go, this was a small one.

Hybrid Musks

Dear Clare,

I think I have solved the problem of my little rose garden, where replanting the exhausted red and white floribundas with new floribundas has not been a success. In spite of digging deep holes and replacing as much of the old soil as possible, the new roses are not thriving – or not all of them. The new floribundas look sickly, but among them I planted three hybrid musks, which have not yet made large bushes but look thoroughly healthy, with clusters of ravishing flowers and, even more important, clean green leaves which have not got blackspot.

The hybrid musks are a godsend to gardeners with less than perfect soil for roses. They were bred by one of the many gardening parsons of the late nineteenth century, the Rev Joseph Pemberton, who resigned from the ministry after thirty-four years to concentrate on roses. In the 1920s, having crossed musk roses over many years with hybrid teas, polyanthas and others, he named this special breed Hybrid Musks. They are shrub roses, tall, graceful and arching (most of them grow to five or six feet), with clusters of charming, unsophisticated flowers in a range of pink, peach and apricot colours, with a few white varieties. They have a musky scent, bloom for a long period, and have strong constitutions. Being much larger plants than my floribundas, I think that four or five plants in each of my four square beds, instead of eight, will be quite enough, and I plan to replace the remaining floribundas with these easier roses in the autumn.

Now for some names. One of my favourites is Penelope, with masses of semi-double lightly-scented flowers in soft coral-pink. I also have Cornelia, which is copper-pink, and a rose bred in 1939 by other specialists after Mr Pemberton's death, Buff Beauty, which is perhaps the finest of all. It is fully double, richly scented, and of what I would call apricot colour, rather than buff, which makes me think of government envelopes. Two good white varieties are Moonlight and Pax. If I get these, the rose garden will no longer be red and white, but a blend of pink, apricot and white, with the green of plentiful leaves.

The bushes should be summer-pruned after the first flowering, and pruned seriously in February or March. Like all cluster roses, they are not good for cutting, so roses for the house must be planted somewhere else. Hybrid musks are often successfully used for rose hedges.

Out of My Class
from Hatfield House

Dearest C,

My panelled and tapestried bedroom looks over the great parterre of twelve square beds edged with clipped box and filled with shrub roses, lilies, pinks and mounds of herbaceous plants. Beyond is a maze fashioned out of yew, then a lake and a beech wood in the distance. In the terrace below me, ladies and gentlemen of impeccable lineage and elegant mien talk politics or gardening and sip a last cup of coffee before beginning the activities of the day. I, the idlest guest, have had my breakfast in bed on a tray decorated with a jug of daisies. In other words, this is the life for me.

To be serious, I have come to do my bit at the annual Festival of Gardening at Hatfield, home of the Salisbury family, where there are marquees of flowers and crafts and fine plants for sale, where a band will soon strike up (I do like a band), and a master of ceremonies will announce a programme of sporting events, competitions, gardening lectures and quizzes, and tours of the Jacobean mansion. This is Sunday, the second day, and my task is to take part in three sessions of a *Gardener's Question Time*, two yesterday and one today.

In the sessions yesterday, two topics prevailed: the first, naturally, was problems arising from the prolonged hot, dry weather. The second, less predictably, was the subject of trees and hedges. Luckily, we had two tree men on the panel, Hugh Johnson and a tree nurseryman, James Chichester, so the questioners got full value. I learned a lot myself, and pass on a few nuggets.

What would the panel suggest for a fast-growing hedge? The most interesting answer was beech, which the experts maintained is not nearly as slow-growing as is commonly thought. I myself suggested yew on the same grounds. Plant yew in enriched soil and feed it with dried blood, and you will get a fine hedge in a very few years, as I found at Rose Cottage, where the hedges look positively ancestral.

Could the panel recommend a quick-growing tree to sit under in the not too distant future? Of several suggestions, the *Malus*, or apple, family won the day, ranging from my own proposal of *Malus floribunda* to an edible crab, such as John Downie. My choice was scorned as a tree being too much of a thicket, but I maintained that if you stripped the lower branches the mushroom head would provide good shade, and I criticised the crab as being too upright to make an umbrella. We all agreed that many eating apple trees would be suitable, as the shade they provide is dappled, not too solid.

A question which came up in both sessions was how to grow oleanders, an increasingly popular shrub which is a fast grower, easy and healthy, flowering over a long period. The experts recommended that you grow your oleander in a tub, not in the ground, preferably on wheels or castors, so that it can be kept under glass in winter and wheeled outdoors for the summer, where it would benefit from the fresh air, sunlight and rain. Starve it, they said, since it is not a shrub which likes rich food. I have seen it growing wild in rocky gulleys in Greece and the Middle East.

We did not have as many questions as usual about roses, though one lady wanted suggestions for a rose hedge. I proposed a *Rosa gallica*, like *Rosa mundi*, for a low hedge, or a hybrid musk for a taller hedge. Most gallica roses are almost thornless, which helps with the clipping. No dissent.

Another hedge question was when to clip box. Lady Salisbury, our hostess, was asked to chip in here as the box hedges at Hatfield can be measured in miles rather than yards. She said that the box was usually clipped three times a year when young to make the small plants bush out, then twice a year at any time from May to late August, but not later, as soft young growth might be nipped by an early frost.

So you see that I have been spending a useful and practical weekend as well as a luxurious one. This is a house where everybody cares deeply about gardening, where the garden is rich in history but is planted with a magical mixture of the best flowers from all the centuries, and where the public is welcome and appreciative. I am lucky to have a share in this fiesta, but you will find me rather deflated next weekend, what with the washing up and my wretched little patch.

July

The Friendly Wasp

Dear Clare,

A subject at the Hatfield *Question Time* which has stuck in my mind is that of pests, which are diabolical this year, in both the greenhouse and the garden. Several of the questioners expressed a dislike of using chemicals, a feeling which is growing in intensity. The panel (I kept quiet for once) discussed the pros and cons of 'biological pest control', which means introducing predators and parasites to kill the pests. First you have to know which particular predator will fancy the pest which is troubling you; for instance, greenhouse whitefly can be controlled by a parasitic wasp called *Encarsia formosa*, and the red spider mite by another mite called *Phytoseiulus persimilis*. These useful creatures can be bought commercially and using them is a high-tech process; the temperature, humidity, number of predators per plant, and so on, have to be monitored with precision. It is obviously not for you or me – I could not manage insect-handling any more than lion-taming, and Calypso gets shamefully hysterical when she sees a wasp – but as the 'green' movement grows so, surely, will this method of pest control which imitates nature.

Out of doors, biological control is even more difficult than under glass as the predators may fly away or lose interest in their prescribed diet, but it is already being used in agriculture in the United States and South America. It sometimes happens naturally in our gardens, as when there is an explosion of ladybirds which feed on greenfly, though I have never found that they eat enough to make much difference. Perhaps scientists will breed a larger and greedier kind of ladybird.

But though the amateur gardener will continue to spray pests, he may prefer to use a non-chemical spray, and the panel recommended soap-and-water. You can buy ready-made sprays labelled '100% bio-degradable', whatever that may mean, or make up your own with pure soap flakes and tepid water. Where only a few plants are infested, I learned that is is more effective to sponge the insects off the leaves and buds, rather than spray them, especially if the infestation is underneath the leaves – a disgusting process, but killing even the nastiest creature is unattractive.

Although I could never attempt it myself, I have written this ill-digested account of biological pest control because it is going to be part of gardening in the future, and I find it fascinating. Also it could be much cheaper than chemical spraying. I will definitely try soap-and-water on the greenfly which are murdering my honeysuckles, and must steel myself to sponge the whitefly off the leaves of my *Helleborus corsicus*. Whitefly used to be mainly a greenhouse pest, but there is another species which can infest the outdoor garden.

Children on the Job

Dearest Clare,

I think Calypso is trapped again, a willing slave of the garden. On Sunday, she and Becky arrived at the cottage before breakfast and spent the morning making an enchanting miniature garden in an old baking tin which I must have given her months ago. There is a bed of soil edged with stones bordering on a silver foil lake. The trees are sprigs of Irish yew, the shrubs are clumps of moss, the flowers are heads picked off potentillas and geraniums, all convincingly in scale. Their total concentration on the work of art they were making was a joy to see, and so was their ingenuity when the soil kept seeping into the lake, making it muddy; I was most impressed that they found a way of keeping it out with a concealed bank of foil.

I think very few children will take a sustained interest in gardening all through childhood. Sports, clothes, pop music, computers, exams or the opposite sex will distract their attention as the years rush by. But while they are still small and loving, children like doing what their parents do, and Calypso has seen the enjoyment which you and I take in planting, feeding, watering, training climbing plants, and so on, and much of it has rubbed off. Even if she forgets the whole thing in her teens, later still, when she is grown up and has a first garden of her own, some misty memory of the pleasure of growing things will give her a head-start over the gardener without any background, just as children who have spoken a second language, and forgotten it, can pick it up again in later years.

If and when Calypso gets tired of gardening, bear it calmly, it will be the sheer pressure of other interests. She already has an eye for choosing colours and grouping plants. This will not pass.

Eye Stoppers

Dear Clare,

When I returned to my normal habitat I found the garden looking remarkably pretty, for there had been just enough rain to freshen it up. The main border is crammed with flowers, but there are too many feathery flowers – alchemilla, geraniums, galega, astrantias and so on. There is a vague mist of colour but no large, solid flowers of strong personality to stop the eye. The delphiniums have fine heads, but are too short this year to do themselves justice, owing to the drought – the giant delphiniums which I saw last week in several Oxford college gardens must have been lavishly watered. If only somebody would breed a long-flowering peony or Oriental poppy it would fill the bill.

Perhaps the answer is one or two shrub roses in the border. I do not really like borders consisting entirely of herbaceous plants, but prefer the occasional solid weight of a shrub or shrub rose. I might plant two important roses, probably rugosas, like the crimson Roseraie de l'Hay, with vivid leaves as well as flowers. And I could have more lilies as eye stoppers, *Lilium regale* does so well here. Later, when the *Sedum* Autumn Joy makes its huge flowerheads, there is no problem.

A friendly thrush has nested in the *Clematis montana* by the back door. It is very late in the season for nests, presumably it is a second brood, and the eggs have hatched, but I tremble for the chicks when they tumble out of the nest and start hopping about, for there was a magpie swooping about early on Sunday morning. I thought of asking Nick to pepper the holly tree where the magpie lurks, but it is full of collared turtle doves, pretty coo-ing birds, so it cannot be done. I did not use the back door at all at the weekend for fear of frightening the thrushes with too much human clatter. If the chicks are stolen I shall cry, like Lesbia over her sparrow, for I mind fearfully – the thrushes trusted me, nesting so near.

Doll's-house Clematis

Dear Clare,

Whoosh. Roses, delphiniums, philadelphus, helianthemums, foxgloves, yellow loosestrife, alliums, honeysuckles and most of the permanent denizens of my garden have collapsed *en masse* in the heat, advancing my usual August dearth of flowers by a whole month. But one glorious group of flowers has come to my rescue, my clematis. They revel in the good drainage and limy soil, and I can count on flowers for many weeks to come. I urge you to plant more of them. At present your only clematis is the pink *Clematis montana* which is rooted in *my* garden, but which you have enticed by witchcraft to climb over the fence and flower on your side.

My large-flowered hybrid clematis are now bravely taking over the torch from the blowsy roses, but I am even fonder of the small-flowered species of both spring and summer, including the native Traveller's Joy C. *vitalba*, which ramps so exuberantly in our chalky woods and hedges and seeds in the garden. Geoffrey Grigson, in his immortal *The Englishman's Flora*, gives thirty-five vernacular names for the plant, including Old Man's Beard, Smoking Cane, Devil's Guts, Hagrope, Honesty and Virgin's Bower, so it seems to have inspired country people of the past with conflicting emotions. Grigson himself saw it as slightly sinister, 'a devil's twister which can twist and choke trees to death, and turn a south-country copse into an Amazonian forest', but he was always a whimsical fellow.

My garden species, though some come from such wild parts of the globe as the Caucusus, Siberia or Tibet, have proved adaptable immigrants, and most of them have been models of behaviour, though C. *montana* is admittedly a bit of a bully. My earliest is C. *macropetala*, with light blue nodding doll's-house flowers in spring and fresh green lace-like leaves. It looks well growing near something yellow, perhaps a broom. At this moment there is an early rush of

late-flowering species, some deep yellow, others, called
viticella clematis, in a range of purples and reds. Two
easy-to-grow yellow species are C. *tangutica* from China,
with flowers like little swinging lanterns, and C. *orientalis*
from Tibet, with nodding bell flowers composed of four
sepals of so thick a texture that it has been given the
nickname of 'lemon-peel clematis'. Both these have fluffy
seedheads, the earliest forming while the later flowers are
still in bloom, making a spontaneous flower arrangement.

Of the viticellas, I have the single C. *v.* Etoile Violette,
with violet flowers and creamy anthers in the centre, and the
double C. *v.* Elegans Plena, which is reddish-purple and
double, an old-fashioned species which was a favourite of
Vita Sackville-West at Sissinghurst. I once had a curious one
with green-and-white flowers called C. *v.* Alba Luxurians
which was given me by Mrs Fish, but sadly I lost it after a few
years – I think it grew through too vigorous a shrub which
overwhelmed it. Another species which I ought to have, but
haven't, is C. *flammula*, with masses of tiny white flowers
with an almond scent. Most of these late species flower into
October and contribute richly to the autumn garden, com-
bining happily with berries and with leaves beginning to turn
colour.

Large-flowered Clematis

Dear Clare,

As you know, I am always a pushover for the wild species of the plant world, and in my last letter I singled out the small-flowered clematis for their childlike charm. But of course I appreciate the brilliance of the large-flowered hybrids. They have a sense of theatre. You do not need to approach them in intimate friendship to enjoy them for they hail you from far away, and have the outgoing personalities which my garden, so full of small flowers, sometimes seems to lack. They come in astonishing colours, sometimes with striped sepals and contrasting stamens which give the wheel-like flowers a central hub.

I won't give you a boring list of names for you can find them well described in numerous catalogues, but I pick out three spectacular beauties which flower over a very long period. Mrs Cholmondeley is the one you have admired climbing through the copper-coloured Emily Gray rambler rose by my back door. The flowers are mid-blue and absolutely huge and bloom from May to September, and I can't think of many flowers which go on for sixteen weeks, except, perhaps, the hellebores in winter. The President in my garden blooms continuously from June to September, a purplish blue with a paler stripe on each sepal and yellow stamens, and the most popular hybrid ever bred, C. *jackmanii* Superba, of royal purple with creamy stamens, lasts almost as long. It is the one on my garden shed.

I don't personally find the cultivation of hybrid clematis much of a problem – they are difficult only in waterlogged or very acid soil – you just plant them carefully in a large hole filled with a richly manured and crumbly soil. But choosing the site does need deep thought. Most clematis flower best in the sun or in light shade, but the roots must be kept shaded and moist, and if there is no natural shade at your chosen spot you must cover the roots with a paving stone or mulch.

Then, what sort of support are you going to give them? A wall, trellis or pergola is fine for a formally trained plant. If you like to see your clematis scramble, you can try to train it through a shrub, but often it seems not to fancy the shrub you have chosen and tries to escape, probably to get more light, and if the shrub is too vigorous it will lose heart and die. I think I like clematis best growing on a wall through a climbing or rambler rose, for roses and clematis seem to be natural friends. The clematis will climb up the strong rose branches of its own accord, needing no help except an occasional tie.

The pruning time varies according to the flowering season, but this is so perfectly explained in the catalogue of Treasures of Tenbury, with the correct pruning time for every plant in the list, that I couldn't compete.

French Gardens

Dear Clare,

I have just received my author's copy of the French edition of *Best Plants*. Two of my books have been translated into Japanese, and very curious they look, but this is my first translation into French, and I feel quite proud of it. I always thought the *The Best Plants for Your Garden* was a flat title, but *Les Plus Belles Plantes de Jardin* has a certain allure. I wonder what the French will make of it, who will buy it, and to what regions of France it might appeal. I can't see its use in the south, for the book is mostly about hardy plants, not the sub-tropicals which make a stage set of the Riviera.

French gardening is either brilliant or catastrophic. There is not the high norm achieved by hundreds of thousands of gifted gardeners in this country. In France, the best gardens are, and always have been, the grand ones, culminating in the architectural triumphs of Le Nôtre at Vaux-le-Vicomte and Fontainebleau which inspire delight ennobled by awe. Nothing here for the little man to copy. And in France it is the forest trees, not the small ornamental trees, which are a joy, especially the avenues of planes or poplars which shade the roads approaching every town and village, and the pollarded planes which canopy the market squares.

Remember Aix to which, meaning well (fatal words), I sent you on leaving school to take a French course at the university? The highly recommended lady to whose house I took you, who was said to have been a heroine of the Resistance, seemed a pillar of respectability, promising good food and comfort and a lift every day to your classes in town. In the event, you were frozen and half-starved, and had to walk to and from Aix running the gauntlet of bolshie students and drunk sailors from Marseilles. I can remember one of my telegrams to you word for word: 'Take taxis everywhere, move to hotel in Aix if necessary, loads of money on the way', to which you replied, 'No go, the

taxi-drivers are gropers to a man.' The limit came when the
university and all its classes closed, as it was the year of
student riots all over France, and I swiftly brought you home.
But in spite of this, you have been back to Aix over and over
again and love its beauty – and its magnificent trees.

The other glory of French gardening is the vegetable
section, so perfectly cultivated that pretentious English
gardeners now call their vegetable patches *potagers*, justified
by a bit of box edging and a couple of *espalier* apples or pears.

But it is a relief to find something which the French do not
do well, and French suburban gardens are dreadful, not only
unimaginative but incompetent. A dwarf weeping willow is
mandatory in the front garden, with a few hybrid tea roses
and marigolds, and some scruffy grass. Worse still is French
municipal planting. A public square in a town is just the
place for formal planting, witness the splendid displays in
English public gardens and in the London parks, but the
French municipal gardener seems to plant any old thing
anyhow. I would single out for vilification the open spaces at
Chartres, where meaningless arrangements of pansies and
wallflowers are peppered with the odd daffodil or hyacinth in
spring, similar jumbles of bedding plants with the occasional
canna lily in summer. I would prefer a full-blown *parterre de
broderie*, which you still sometimes find in Italian provincial
towns.

I am looking forward hugely to staying in Provence in
August, where I will poke my inquisitive nose over French
garden gates and hedges, and will file a report, and please
report back on the gardens of your mountain holiday in
Spain. Oh dear, I will miss our annual family outing, and
beloved Calypso's conversation, but this summer invitations
have drawn us in different directions.

August

A *Wicked Month*

Dear Clare,

August has been called a wicked month, and it can certainly be so in the garden. I was full of curiosity on Sunday when Betty Hussey and I drove over from Scotney to Sissinghurst to see what that great garden could do in the harshest month of the year. We went in the early evening when the crowds had gone and the light was beginning to soften. Having spent so many happy hours there years ago writing my Sissinghurst book, I still feel a special relationship with the garden, and Nigel emerged from the house when we arrived to chat and explain the presence of a BBC camera crew – they are filming *Portrait of a Marriage*, with a script by Penelope Mortimer.

I am delighted to say that the garden is a triumph. The only sign of drought is that the grass is brownish, for hosing is banned, but otherwise it is resplendent, almost tropical in the brilliance of the flowers.

The clematis which curtain the ancient walls of small, mellow, hand-made bricks, are now at their peak, but as I have written a lot about clematis lately I will just add that I had no idea of the variety of small-flowered clematis which are available, nodding their little heads in every shade of blue, pink, purple, yellow and white. Some are bi-coloured, like C. *campaniflora*, which has white bell flowers suffused with blue; some are scented, like the ravishing Chinese species, C. *aethusifolia*, with bell flowers of palest yellow.

Of the ten enclosed gardens which make up Sissinghurst, the best at this time is the Front Courtyard with its Purple Border; this has clematis and purple-leaved vines on the background wall, and late-flowering herbaceous plants in the bed itself. There are clumps and pools of thistly plants – the giant purple cardoon, *Cynara cardunculus*, and the spiny *Eryngium tripartitum* with grey-blue globe flowers. There are red and blue salvias, a lilac-pink bergamot called Beauty of

Cobham, a few late delphiniums, and drifts of heliotrope and violas at the border's edge. Many of the plants here are hardy perennials, and we could all grow them and have better August gardens if we were not so obsessed with the flowers of spring.

The Cottage Garden is also at its zenith, but many of the plants here are tender and reared in the greenhouse, and are out of our range. This enclosure has always had a theme of red, yellow and orange flowers, and on Sunday evening it was glowing like hot coals, with dahlias, red hot pokers, red crocosmia, the scarlet *Lobelia cardinalis* and huge-leaved crimson tropical cannas.

There is not a great deal at Sissinghurst for the small-time gardener to imitate, so great are the gardeners' resources, but it is inspiring to see such a masterpiece of the gardener's art.

Dear M,

Back from Spain, and Emma's delicious house, and a triumph of August gardening fit to match Sissinghurst. After the humidity of London it was a relief to arrive in Malaga and find the atmosphere so much fresher. The journey went like a breeze, everything on time, luggage not lost, and the drive down the coast road achieved in the dark – it is essential to do the drive at night as the road is so ugly. The Spanish are intent on filling every gap with another concrete block which never gets finished. All the trees and plants are

covered with a thick layer of dust and I longed to get hold of
a hose and water them down. Greenness and tranquillity are
only to be found when you take the turning up into the hills,
towards the doll's-house village and Casa Emma.

When we arrived, the outgoing guests had just started
dinner on the top terrace, and our calls of 'cooee, we're here'
were greeted with gasps of shock and horror. Emma had
thought we were arriving the next day. Never mind. Calypso
had a restful night on the swimming pool mattress.

The garden is to die for. The house is built around an
ancient tiled courtyard, with bedrooms and terraces to be
discovered up and down various wiggly staircases. There are
several eating, drinking and sitting areas, each with its own
view across the neatly terraced hillside. Emma has packed
the courtyard with plants, and the evening scent of the
jasmine wafts everywhere.

At Casa Emma everything grows abundantly, helped by
guests watering each evening. Roses, philadelphus, bougain-
villea, hibiscus, grapes, wisteria all flowering, shooting and
swelling at a gratifying rate. Morning glory floods over the
back walls and large canna lilies loom from terracotta pots.
Daily fights are waged against the ants while Emma carries
out an eccentric evening ritual with a metal pole to terrify
the swallows that sit in the pear tree and make messes over
the tile flooring. It is Emma's pride and joy, so much so that
it must be shared with everybody. The large double front
door is left open day and night and passing locals and tourists
cluster round enviously, peering through to the leafy green
beyond.

I shall miss it. So will Calypso. When brother Max beefs
on about children (thinking of himself) preferring Frinton to
foreign parts, he doesn't take account of his niece. Her
pleasure in everything from the local bread shop to the walks
up the mountains (we gathered wild herbs for her school
project and pressed oleander flowers) is prodigious. We have
hardly got back from this holiday and she is already discussing the next. As am I.

Wild Creatures

Dear C,

It was an edifying sight to see you spot a mole crossing your lawn this morning and catching it with your gloved hands. Then came the problem, what to do with it? You did the only possible thing in setting it free in the waste patch across the road which is riddled with moles. I thought they understood their place and I do not know how it got into your garden. I do not think it would have crossed the road – unlike the poor hedgehogs, moles do not seem addicted to road travel – but if they are beginning to tunnel *under* the road, and arrive in droves, you will be in for trouble.

This raises the whole question of wildlife in the garden. Does one encourage it, tolerate it, or attack it if it becomes a serious nuisance? Christopher Lloyd, who has more to lose than we have, is understandably hawkish, and says 'one cannot really expect a good garden and a menagerie all in the same plot.' Bigoted conservationists, on the other hand, would have us sleep with bats in the bedroom and cultivate nettles to feed the caterpillars of the Small Tortoiseshell butterfly. Not me. I suppose it must be a matter of compromise.

Some animals are so pestilential that I think they must be harshly dissuaded, especially rabbits. I am alarmed at the population explosion of muntjac deer, which have already arrived from other counties and munched their way through gardens only three miles away, and I hope that forceful characters, like the farmers, will try to keep them down. (What we need is an old-fashioned village poacher, a dying breed. Our local genius, now long deceased, used to knock down the roosting pheasants at night with a catapult.) But what about mice? I feel that the garden is as much their home as mine, and do not grudge them a few seeds, though I do set traps among the cyclamen, they eat the corms. Hedgehogs are welcome. So are bees, but not wasps. So are all birds except pigeons and members of the crow family, and if the crows would leave me just one basket of my walnuts, I would give them the rest, but they pick the tree clean. I used to reproach the eighteenth-century diarist, Parson Wood-forde, in my mind for shooting a woodpecker in his garden but, on reading the passage again, I found that the bird was destroying his thatch, so it is hard to blame him.

The trouble with wild animals is that they have no idea of give and take. We are prepared to share our garden with them, but they give no thought for us. I offer no cut-and-dried solution to the dilemma. It is something to think and talk about. Incidentally, we are not the first generation to wonder how much licence to give wild creatures in the garden. Joseph Addison, writing in 1712, said that his neighbours were amazed that he allowed so many birds, but 'I value my garden more for being full of birds than cherries, and very frankly give them fruit for their songs'.

Dear M,

At least with you the wildlife remains where nature intended, firmly ensconced in the garden. At Bankside, during the first signs of a chilly evening, they pack their bags and start the short march up into the snugness of the thatch roof, nice and warm, with food on tap. One night in the not too distant future I will be lying blissfully in bed when my peace will be shattered by the patter of tiny feet scuttling from one end of the rafters to the other. As winter progresses, the tiny feet give way to bigger ones and the invasion is on.

Like you, I am happy to share my living quarters with the odd bird. Blue tits nested in the eaves this year, and from my bedroom window I watched the parents sitting beadily on the telephone wires waiting for a safe moment to deliver lunch. I draw the line at mice and rats. The only access to the roof is via the eaves, and once a year we call in the big guns in the shape of Newbury District Council. They arrive and push packages of poison into the roof and round the barn. I dread to imagine the horrors of the burial chamber, and the mass of accumulating corpses.

I'm afraid the mole I captured had a nest of young concealed under the kitchen step – I spotted them scuttling from under the polyanthus leaves back to the safety of the bricks. Calypso would like me to capture them all so that they can grow up with the hamster, but I am neither St Francis nor Joan of Arc.

Big Vegetables

Dear Clare,

I have not eaten a runner bean this year, although I bought two pounds of stringy brick-hard monsters last week which I had to throw away. I have only once eaten broad beans, and that was by courtesy of my friend in Kent who grows her own and picks them in infancy. Could you not possibly grow a bean or two next season? I used to grow delicate little broad beans which nestled in their felty wombs until they were half an inch long, when I picked them and cooked them for two to three minutes. This early picking encourages more beans to fatten, so I doubt if the crop is lighter in the long run.

The preoccupation with size among market gardeners and even amateurs who ought to know better is a disaster for the cook, and I cannot help thinking that the flower and produce shows which are now being held all over the country are partly to blame. There ought to be an extra class for infant vegetables, or perhaps a tasting of cooked vegetables by judges like Elizabeth David.

Competition growers all through history have gone for size. The winning gooseberry of all time was grown in Staffordshire in 1852, weighed just over two ounces, and was about the size of a small tomato. The variety was 'London', which is still popular, and it was champion in a match between two local teams for a prize of ten shillings. Today, vegetables are officially judged by criteria other than size – onions should have slender necks and parsnips strong shoulders – but the winning exhibits do seem to be elephantine. What would one *do* with an onion the size of a football? Or a 2-foot-long leek?

The tricks which over-ambitious competitors get up to confirm that size is more important than the organisers claim. It is possible to enlarge a vegetable marrow by making a small hole near the stalk and inserting a piece of string, with the other end in a bowl of water, a sort of intravenous feeding. This is against the rules, as is the polishing of onions to give them a shine or the bleaching of potatoes to whiten them, but it is not unknown, so a judge has to be a bit of a detective as well as having a practised eye for perfect shape, clear colour, and uniformity between the five or seven specimens grouped artistically on a dish.

Could you somehow find space for three short rows of Aquadulce broad beans to be sown in November? A cottage garden without broad beans is unworthy of the name. If Nick could dig the ground, I will barrow down some manure, and you could fork it in. *And somehow I will sow them*, crawling along on my knees. I claim this job for myself because I know that you will never bother to use a line, and the rows must be straight or they are nothing. These beans, autumn sown, mature early, say in mid-June, when none of us will be on holiday, and we will eat them with a piece of gammon (beans and bacon are an ancient peasant tradition) and a jug of parsley sauce, and we will invite nobody but the family so that we can have a feast.

Only the Best

Dearest Clare,

Why does one ever go anywhere but to France? Our mill-house in Provence was unspoiled perfection. But holidays have one nasty aftermath in that one views everything on return with alarmingly clear eyes. Looking at the garden, I ask myself whether it is from laziness or sentimentality that I have slipped into tolerating too many plants which are second-rate. Why haven't I cast them on the rubbish heap and chosen better varieties? Vita Sackville-West always urged gardeners to 'grow only the best', and she abolished inferior forms of plants or second-rate hybrids if better ones came along. I know it is difficult when one has put a lot of care into a plant to admit that it is a failure, but it is pointless to struggle on. After all, a plant is not a baby, to be accepted for better or worse.

But, you may say, what makes a good plant, and how are you to know it when it is just a name in a catalogue or a puny thing in a pot? The main criteria are its overall shape, the size and colour of the flowers, the quality of the leaves, the length of flowering time and its hardiness and general stamina. You learn the best names by asking and reading – asking professionals and connoisseurs, and reading not only books but expert magazines like *The Garden* and *Country Life* which keep you up-to-date with new improvements and discoveries. To save you the agonies of trial and error, which can mean wasted years in the case of shrubs, I'll name a few plants which are among the élite.

I know you are thinking of a few more shrubs, especially viburnums. I suggest the hybrid *Viburnum burkwoodii* in the form called Park Farm; it has especially large flower clusters which are pink instead of brown in the bud, raising it immediately above the common herd. If you want a winter-flowering viburnum, I think the large-flowered *V. bodnantense* Dawn is a better choice than the *V. farreri* which I have in my own garden, which has the same sweet scent but undersized flowers. For your roof garden in London, do think about a dwarf rhododendron which looks sensational in pots, *R. yakushimanum* Hydon Dawn, with large frilled pink flowers and glossy evergreen leaves which are silver when the shoots are young.

If you have space at the cottage for a new climbing plant, you would revel in the glorious form of *Clematis orientalis* called Bill MacKenzie. The yellow flowers are larger and finer than those of the common species, and bloom for many weeks in late summer and autumn. It makes all the other yellow clematis look rather dim.

Choosing herbaceous plants is not so critical, for you can more easily change them, but even so, it is worth looking for the best. An outstanding Michaelmas daisy is the *Aster frikartii* called Mönch, with starry lavender-blue flowers with large yellow centres. Another special border perennial is *Aconitum napellus* Bressingham Spire, with dark violet flowers. The best *Geranium endressii* for ground cover is A.T. Johnson, the delicate pink flowers having a silvery sheen. If you want a tall form of Solomon's seal for cutting, look for *Polygonatum majalis* Fortin's Giant, though I prefer the smaller native species out-of-doors.

These are only a tiny handful of 'best plants' to give you a taste of the idea, but in almost every category from trees to rock plants there are a few star plants which outshine the rest.

Small Beginnings

Dear Clare,

The garden is bursting with seeds, some already ripe, such as those of my favourite member of the parsley tribe, *Smyrnium perfoliatum*, and Calypso has been collecting them in screw-top jars. Other seeds which are ripe, or nearly so, are those of love-in-a-mist, sweet scabious, astrantia, *Limnanthes douglasii* (the poached-egg plant), and the ravishing old-fashioned sweet pea called Matucana, with small purple-and-violet flowers and a heavenly scent. We could sort them into envelopes and sow them in the spring, but the *Smyrnium*, sweet peas, love-in-a-mist, astrantia and *Limnanthes* could be sown in the open within the next few weeks, say, until mid-November, with some oxlip seeds which I saved a few weeks back.

You can, of course, broadcast these seeds in suitable beds and wild corners, but in a jumbled garden like yours and mine many will be lost in the crowd. If they do germinate, it is all too easy to pull out the seedlings by mistake when you are weeding, especially if you cannot tell the seed-leaves of a tree peony from Herb Robert, if I may be really catty. It is better to sow the seeds in a seedbed and mark them, and to move them in the spring.

I have an idea for Calypso which I think would not be an imposition, but which she would enjoy. Could you dig for her a very small seedbed in which she could sow the seeds which she is collecting? Just a decent bit of soil in a sunny spot, well-raked and smooth. I will give her a packet of labels and a pen and help her to write out the names of the seeds to mark each little row. She cannot fail to get some results next year. Incidentally, I have spotted in my rose garden a strong self-sown seedling of the yellow *Paeonia ludlowii* you wanted, and you can have it in the autumn.

Propagating is a satisfying form of gardening – you feel an almost maternal happiness when your seed or cutting grows into an independent plant. To propagate seriously one must have a greenhouse or a cold frame, but even without these amenities one can do some simple propagating out of doors, not only sowing seeds but taking cuttings. For instance, 4-inch cuttings of woody sub-shrubs, like lavender and sage, can be taken now: choose strong non-flowering shoots and pinch out the tips and plant them in an open bed with a handful of mixed sand and peat underneath to encourage roots to form. Peter Robinson next door grew his splendid lavender hedge from cuttings of my Old English Lavender which he planted directly into the site, and I believe there was not a single failure.

Some larger shrubs, such as buddleia and philadelphus, can also be propagated in the open from hardwood cuttings (i.e. ripe wood), about 10 inches long. Take these in October or November and plant them in a peat-and-sand soil mixture in the same way, but do not expect them to root for a year or more.

This is all very elementary, and if you got keen it would be best to invest in a frame, but much can be done without one. Osbert achieved some deutzia and phlomis plants which are now serious features in the garden by taking outdoor cuttings, and was immensely proud of them. Apart from the fun of it, it is gratifying to get plants for free.

September

First Bookshelf

Dearest Child,

One for facts, one for ideas, one for amusement, one for ecstasy. I have been pondering on which four books I would choose for a learner-gardener's bookshelf, assuming that the beginner, though ignorant of gardening, would be otherwise literate.

As a reference book of facts, the *Reader's Digest Encyclopaedia of Garden Plants and Flowers* was formerly unique, and mine is falling apart from use. But now there is a newer blockbuster, the *R.H.S. Gardeners' Encyclopaedia of Plants and Flowers*, edited by the incomparable Chris Brickell. This lists 8,000 plants, classified according to their function in the garden, shrubs, climbers, perennials, rock plants, and so on, with colour photographs, descriptions and growing instructions, and breaks new ground by marking every plant for hardiness with one, two or three stars. The Reader's Digest volume has fewer plants (3,000), but is easier for quick reference, the plants being listed in ABC order. To have one or the other is essential.

There are many contestants for the book of ideas. Graham Stuart Thomas's *Perennial Garden Plants* ranks very high, for it is not only a dictionary of the best perennials, but is strong on the difficult subject of plant associations (what to plant with what), of which Graham Thomas is a master. Of the golden oldies, V. *Sackville-West's Garden Book* is inspirational, and the modesty with which she writes is heartwarming when you consider how deep was her knowledge and how grand her background; she never patronised, but distilled her experience thoughtfully for the humbler gardener. But my final choice would go to *The Well-Tempered Garden* by Christopher Lloyd, for though the themes are serious, the tone is human and witty.

For amusement, I would choose every time, *Elizabeth and Her German Garden*, by Elizabeth von Arnim, and usually it is out of my bookshelf and beside my bed. Elizabeth was a clever, attractive, waspish young creature who married a bad-tempered German count in 1889 and made a garden on his estate in Prussia. She is cruelly witty about her neighbours, her staff, and particularly her husband, whom she refers to as the Man of Wrath, but she had a genuine passion for nature and for her wildish garden, full of lilacs and roses, poppies and columbines, lavender and pinks, in an isolated countryside of pine forests and cornfields. Though her words are sharp, they have a poetic beauty, so that the book is both a comedy and an idyll.

It could almost count as a book of ecstasy, but I think it would be nice to have one book which would take the reader right out of the garden and into the wild. *On the Eaves of the World*, by Reginald Farrer, does just that. Farrer was a plant-hunter, and when World War One broke out he was exploring in a part of China so remote that it was many months before he heard the news. In beautiful prose, he describes the joys of looking for plants in the wild, making light of the dangers and hardships. When he spots the glorious Moutan Peony in a copse in the mountains he plunges into the scrub as excited as a schoolboy, and when he reaches the peony – 'that enormous single blossom of pure white, with featherings of deepest maroon radiating from the base of the petals' – he remains for a long time quietly worshipping it, before returning 'at last in the dusk in high contentment'.

When looking at the many exotic flowers which are now quite at home in English gardens, it adds to one's appreciation to recall that the botanists who discovered them were as intrepid as Christopher Columbus or Dr Livingstone.

A *Flower* Carpet

Dear Clare,

Treasure trove! It isn't often that one lights upon a totally new idea, but I saw something so fresh and delightful earlier this evening that I can't wait to report it.

I went up to the Hay-Drummonds to collect a basket of figs which Auriol had promised me, and we strolled through the garden where she still has plenty of roses, having kept blackspot at bay by sustained spraying. But even better, outside the drawing-room window, where there used to be a rose-bed which got tired, like mine, she has planted the old bed like a Persian carpet. The planting is absolutely flat, with a loose pattern of creeping jenny (*Lysimachia nummularia*) running into the purple-leaved *Viola labradorica*, both perennial plants, with a few bright splashes of busy lizzie (*Impatiens* varieties), which is of course a bedding plant. The busy lizzies will be taken out when the frosts turn them brown, and be replaced with forget-me-nots for spring. The ground is solid with flowers and leaves, none of them more than three or four inches high. Most of the plants are permanent and ramble freely, there is none of the geometric stiffness of 'carpet bedding'. The only planting I have seen which at all resembles it is a thyme lawn, made with thyme in pink, purple and white.

Auriol is an exceptionally creative gardener. We have all agreed that there is no cook to compare with her in Berkshire, and her knowledge of English porcelain is exhaustive. Now she reveals this additional gift. I think there is quite a future in the flat bed planted freely, with the plants going their own way, not regimented as in a French *parterre*. The upkeep is minimal, and the plants are so closely interwoven that weeds don't stand a chance.

What other plants could one use in the flowery carpet? Possibly clover, ajuga or bugle, creeping campanulas, like *C. cochlearifolia* in blue or white, even creeping miniature roses

– the alpine catalogues would be the ones to suggest ideas for plants which form a mat. I must ask Auriol if she uses bulbs in the carpet, for dwarf narcissi or tulip species would look delightful, especially the striped tulips which have such an air of Turkey, Persia, Bokhara and all the carpet countries. The splashes of bedding plants could be changed from year to year according to fancy.

The site chosen would have to be quite flat and sunny so that all the plants would grow at the same pace.

September Pink

Dear Clare,

I arrived at the cottage wondering, as I braved my way on the M4 between the juggernauts on the left and the BMWs on the right (at least the juggernaut men know how to drive), whether I would find the garden yellow with the last of the summer daisy plants or red with berries and turning leaves. It is neither. Most of the flowers are a tender pink. One forgets that a band of pink separates August and October.

There are clouds of pink Japanese anemones standing on tall, straight stalks which need no stake. I like to mix them in vases with sprays of variegated dogwood. The nerines have burst into flower since my last visit two weeks ago, enough of them to spare a bunch for the house which I will take up to London on Sunday, for they last well and do not wilt on the journey. The hedges are bright with the pink berries of wild spindle.

The Autumn Joy sedums make huge pink clumps and have not yet turned tawny – every phase of this plant is good, from the early tight green clusters of leaves to the chocolate brown of the flowerheads in winter. There has been plenty of rain which has brought a revival of the pink snapdragons which, in company with white tobacco plant, are among the best bedding plants in this garden. And there are a few pink roses, the shell-pink of the hybrid musk Felicia, and a second flowering of the deep, almost magenta, pink of the bourbon Mme Isaac Perèire. If I look at them from a distance I don't see the blackspot.

Most appealing of all is the drift of *Cyclamen hederifolium* among the shrubs, especially dear to me because I remember the bunches of cyclamen which friends sent to my bedside when you were born, some of them mixed with gentians, a happy pairing. I have been reading with horror that in Turkey the wild cyclamen are being decimated to feed the Dutch commercial market, which they often reach in a dying condition, past salvation. Cyclamen are easily grown from seed, and indeed seed themselves here freely, though it is best to pot up the seedlings and nurture them for a year until they are strong enough to fend for themselves in the open ground. If you want to move cyclamen, you should do it when the corms are growing, not dormant, and as soon as mine have finished flowering I will give you a few to start a drift of your own. They like leaf-mouldy soil, and the loveliest I have ever seen were growing wild in woods near Asolo, in northern Italy, where we used to stay with Freya Stark. In addition to her rarer talents, she was an impassioned gardener.

Autumn Orders

Dear Clare,

I spent most of Tuesday at the RHS Great Autumn Show, looking in particular for a few border plants to order now and plant as soon as they arrive, praying that they come within a few weeks while the soil is still warm. Nothing gives one so much confidence as choosing plants in the flesh, and I placed two small orders for plants which, though not at all rare, I haven't grown before, one for crocosmias and one for *Aster lateriflorus*, and I will tell you why.

When I was young there used to be a dreary orange plant of the iris family, much grown in sooty London gardens, called montbretia. It went out of fashion, and though some good hybrids were produced, they were not very hardy. Now called crocosmia, everyone seems to be growing it because some hardier hybrids have been bred in more attractive colours. They have spikes of flowers which bend over at the top like bluebells. There is a good flame-red called Lucifer and an orange-and-yellow called Vulcan. The nicest is an apricot-yellow called Solfatare, but I am told it is less hardy and you might lose it in a bad winter. Most of the crocosmias flower through August and September and are easy to grow but are, I must warn you, invasive.

Why haven't I been growing any of those later autumn flowers which come out in September and October, the small-flowered Michaelmas daisies? There are several species, including *Aster ericoides* and *A. lateriflorus*, with miniscule flowers which grow in cloud-like sprays, giving the same misty effect as gypsophila in a bed or in a vase with something more substantial, such as dahlias. They are easy to grow and absolutely hardy, modest but lovable plants, like so many daisies. The one I chose is called *A. lateriflorus* Coombe Fishacre, in a pale lilac-pink.

A distaste for Michaelmas daisies is another of my ancient mistakes, because I always associated them with mildew. But these species and their hybrids do not get mildew, nor does the species with large flowers with rayed petals called A. *amellus*, which has many beautiful hybrids, mostly about 2 feet tall with the virtue that they begin to flower in August. Also innocent of mildew are the much taller Michaelmas daisies in the *Aster novae-angliae* or New England range; the villains are the *novii-belgii* group, which are to be avoided. I am currently poring over Bressingham Gardens and other catalogues, because I have been foolish in overlooking these plants for so long.

Small Bulbs

Dear Child,

The ground is still like concrete and it will take days of drenching rain to make it plantable, but one should be at the ready with neat little packets of bulbs to plant when the moment comes.

I suggest that you top up with more small bulbs for many reasons. There is no need to urge their charm, or their accommodating way of filling up odd corners, but there is another advantage – most of them flower early, and die down early, so that their dying leaves are not an eyesore through the summer. The mid-season and late daffodils look pretty unattractive while they wither, and one longs to cut them down too soon for their health.

Though I adore the tall, late-flowering scented narcissus, and also huge, vulgar tulips, especially parrot tulips, I'm thinking at the moment about the small bulbs which delight with their innocence and courage as they push up into a harsh world, often through snow. Many of them are intended for a rock garden, but they are just as beautiful by the front door, or at the foot of a shrub or small deciduous tree where they will not be swamped by the large leaves of herbaceous plants trying to steal the scene.

I don't think you have any dwarf irises; most of them have beautiful markings which deserve close observation when you pick them in bud to open indoors in the dreary days of late winter. One of the earliest is *I. histrioides* Major, a madonna blue iris with gold and white markings on the falls, which often flowers in January. Plant a few by the front door so that you can pick them without having to stump about in your wellies. Next to flower are the many forms of *I. reticulata*, which have a heady scent. I once took my dear friend Lanning Roper a bunch of *Iris histrioides* when he was ill in hospital, and he said, sniffing them, 'I didn't realise these had any scent.' I had slipped in just three *Iris reticulata* which had opened early, and they scented the whole bunch. They have velvety flowers and can be found in many shades of blue, including a dark purple.

On the other side of the door you could plant a few small daffodils, perhaps the 6-inch Tête-à-Tête. And you could try a circle of the Hoop Petticoat daffodil, *Narcissus bulbocodium*, under one of your apple or plum-trees where they will not get lost. The corona is curiously shaped like a funnel. They are naturalised in masses in the alpine meadow at Wisley.

Tulip species are irresistible, especially those with striped petals or leaves which look oriental, as indeed many of them are by origin. *Tulipa greigii* Red Riding Hood is scarlet, with stripy leaves in green and bronze. *Tulipa kauffmanniana* should also be in your collection. The species is from Turkestan, and there are many varieties, of which Heart's Delight, deep pink on the outside and white within, is a favourite of mine. The commended treatment for many tulip species is to lift them in the summer, dry them off and replant them in autumn, but life's too short for such refinements, and most will last for years if you leave them in the ground. I used to grow small tulips in pots in my cold greenhouse and bring them indoors to flower, and I think you might try this in a window, or certainly on your roof garden in London, which gets lots of sun.

The small chrysanthus crocuses are another late winter pleasure, and they flower much earlier than the fat Dutch hybrids. My *C.c.* E.P. Bowles, a lemon yellow crocus with feathery bronze markings at the base of the petals, has made large clumps in the grass, but if you want an early crocus which will increase faster than any other, you should plant a few lavender blue *Crocus tommasinianus* among your shrubs. I am afraid that wind and rain tend to knock them about, but they stand up better as the clumps grow larger.

We will all be a bit late with our bulb planting this year, but the soil is so warm that I am sure they will catch up.

For Planting Now

Dear Clare,

There are not many winter-flowering bedding plants, but one which would please you ought to go in now, the Universal strain of pansies. They are suitable for tubs and pots or as a winter carpet to cheer up the rosebeds. I have bought you three to see if you like them and if you do, you can buy some more at any garden centre, where you can choose the flowers with the most appealing faces. I have bought you one blue one, one yellow, and one white, all with screwed-up pansy faces which seem to be saying 'ouch'. You can get plain colours, too. They will flower in almost any weather but it is vital that you deadhead them, for they must not be allowed to seed; therefore a small planting is more convenient than a large expanse. They will be finished in about April when you take them out and, in due course, replace them with summer bedding plants. The last time I grew them they continued to flower all through the summer, but this was beyond the call of duty.

October

Crumbly Soil

Dear Clare,

I used to love working the soil at this time of year, for forking and weeding and mulching give the same sort of physical pleasure as sifting and pouring and beating the ingredients of a Yorkshire pudding. I might not feel the same if my soil were heavy clay, but as you know it is light and amenable. However, this year the going is tough, and Melanie has been having a hard time breaking the compacted soil of the rosebeds, which solidified in the drought.

If you can get your soil into reasonable condition now, you can quickly plant your bulbs (except for the tulips, which should wait until November), for bulbs are not fussy. Then try to improve the soil further before you plant shrubs or herbaceous things. Frost and rain will help. If you have a new piece of ground to bring into cultivation, the theory is that you dig it and leave the topsoil in lumps for the frost to break up. It will do this beautifully in a hard winter, penetrating every clod with threads of ice, making them crumbly in the spring. But if your ground is fully planted, like mine, deep working will damage the roots of plants, and you just fork between the plants to let in the air and the rain. *And then you must mulch it.*

There are two schools of thought about the season for mulching, some saying that an autumn mulch will be washed away by winter rains. True. But sometimes there is snow on the ground as late as April, and if the mulching is delayed until spring, it may never get done at all. Therefore, I like to see the beds tucked up for winter with an eiderdown of organic stuff, and hope the worms will pull it down.

But what organic stuff? I can count on Bower Farm for manure, and a load of good fat smelly stuff usually lasts me two years. Then there ought to be compost, but I used to put hours of work into making compost and end up with enough to cover a sixpence; now I blush to say that much of the waste which the virtuous gardener composts goes on the bonfire. I do have decayed grass mowings which improve the texture of the soil, but are not very nourishing. My favourite soil food is leaf-mould, and in the good old days the council roadmen used to clear the ditches of leaves and every year would deliver a lorry-load to my gate. Now they have stopped carting leaves, and though the garden provides some leaf-mould of its own, I need more, especially for the cyclamen. Do you think Nick could make up a working party of children, take a pile of sacks, and fill them with leaves from the verges of the woods? There is masses of glorious decayed stuff asking to be collected.

Another mulching material which is recommended *passim* is peat; this does not actually feed the plants, but encourages root growth. Used in quantity, however, it is appallingly expensive, and I have misgivings about the environment. With boggy areas anywhere from Devon to Ireland being stripped of peat, what sort of soil is left behind? It takes centuries for peat to form.

Two of the best gardens I have ever seen made mulching easy for the gardener because the material was always at hand. In Princess Sturdza's garden in Normandy (a paradise of woods and streams and flower-filled clearings) organic material is carted to strategic spots all over the garden and hidden behind trees; farm manure, compost, wood-ash, leaf-mould and peat are always at the ready. And the late Collingwood Ingram, renowned collector of Japanese cherries, had huge stacks of organic food outside his potting-shed. The gardeners just filled their barrows as they set out to plant. Incidentally, 'Cherry' Ingram lived to the age of a hundred and one, mulching to the last.

Rich Compost

Dear Clare,

In my last letter, I think I was somewhat cavalier about garden compost. This is a subject over which I feel guilt, because compost is certainly the best and most natural of garden foods and soil creators, and I am resolving to make more of it, my present heap being amateurish and inefficient. As many different methods of making compost are mooted I thought I would consult the best compost-maker I know, my friend Eric Williams, and I have been to visit him in the Lambourn valley. There the soil, like ours, is light and chalky.

Eric, as you know, is a teacher, and explained his compost method with professional ease. He is not a fanatic on the subject, bowing three times to the moon when he draws from the heap, or any of that rubbish, but just says that compost is the easiest, cheapest and most satisfactory way of feeding all plants, from trees to vegetables.

First we went to look at the heaps. Vital information – there are three of them, and three are essential to provide a proper rotation since compost takes two years to rot down. So there is one new heap, still being added to with autumn material, one half-rotted heap, and one fully rotted for current use. If you have only time, space or material for a limited amount of compost, Eric says you must still have three heaps, even if they are small ones. In Eric's case, there is one huge bin divided into three compartments, but the heaps can be separate if more convenient.

Then he explained the construction of the heaps. They are sited in a shady place so that they will not dry out in summer. The surrounds are solidly constructed of breeze blocks, which are porous, allowing the air and moisture to get in and out. Eric said that wood containers will rot in time, and corrugated iron is not only hideous but has a habit of crumpling or blowing away. His particular bins are very

large, about 6 feet long by 3½ feet wide. In depth, 1½ feet of
soil was dug out when the bins were made, adding to the
above-ground walls made of three rows of breeze blocks. The
three bins are firmly separated by partitions, so that the
different vintages of compost do not get mixed up. They are
not covered, but when one bin is piled high (it will, of
course, sink) a layer of farm manure is put on top as a
covering. Otherwise, nothing is added, such as an activator,
there is none of the backbreaking business of turning the
heap, and there is no watering. You just take the compost
from the top as you need it.

What goes into the heap? Everything except woody
things. Masses of leaves, weeds (except bindweed, couch
grass and similar horrors), grass, dead moss, wood-ash, rotten
apples and household waste. I protested at this, saying that
household rubbish was enough trouble without sorting it and
carting the tea-leaves and vegetable peelings to the distant
heap, but he was firm. He admitted that he had just found a
silver fruit-knife in the mature heap, which must have
escaped from the kitchen three years ago. In that soft, black
crumbly mixture it had been as perfectly preserved as a gold
necklace in a pharaoh's grave.

These heaps provide enough compost to feed the whole
one-acre garden, and nothing else is bought except the
manure to top the heaps and a seed compost for the
greenhouse. The whole garden is mulched with it, all plants
are planted with it, and if once in a way a full-grown tree
should look sickly, the soil beneath it is taken off and
compost put in at root level as a tonic, always with good
results.

As this is one of the few chalk gardens where I have seen
hybrid tea roses grown successfully, the compost must be as
good as it looks, which is good enough to eat.

The Grand Clear-up

Dear Clare,

I can't remember what Freud said about excessively tidy people, I'm sure it was something disagreeable, or am I thinking of Dr Spock and the evils of premature pot-training? As you know, I am an obsessive tidier-up, and I am delighted when the time comes to sweep the leaves, clear the garden rubbish, pull up the untidy stakes which are leaning in all directions, cut down the dead plants, make a mighty bonfire and plead with the mower to cut the grass for perhaps the penultimate time this year. I *love* the garden to be tidy, which mine never is in spring and summer, but soon it will look like a night nursery put to rights by an old-fashioned nanny, with all the plants asleep in their cots. (It must be said that there is an alternative view about the cutting down of herbaceous borders, which I might write about later on.)

The first item on the tidiness agenda will be to have a bonfire of the huge pile of tree prunings which we dared not burn in the drought for fear of igniting your thatch, and later Melanie will spread the wood-ash on the rosebeds. (How good it is, now that some rain has come, to see some worms again, creating new soil. How are you off for worms? If you have none, or only large ones, you must get on with the cultivation of the soil, for the poor things cannot thread their way through solid clods.)

Next on the agenda are the fallen apples. The apple crop was a bumper one, especially of my large crimson eater called Charles Ross, which provided a basketful for the harvest festival. But there are a lot of windfalls which nobody wants, and I must organize a street party to collect and burn them, for they are rotting and attracting flies and wasps. I have picked up the fallen walnuts, which are delicious, but the wretched crows will get the main crop. They crack the nuts up in the trees and gobble them on the spot, littering the ground with shells.

Most of the border plants can now have their stalks cut down, though not too close, but a few plants prefer to keep their leaves as frost protection. Nepeta, or catmint, should not be trimmed too close, nor should the epimediums, and the stems of *Sedum* Autumn Joy should be left until spring, no disadvantage as the brown flowerheads are so handsome.

More controversial are lawns and leaves. I personally believe in cutting grass, though not shaving it, throughout the autumn, and even in winter if it grows excessively, for long grass deprives the roots of oxygen. Besides, my grass grows unevenly and long tufts are an eyesore, and if the orchard grass grows high the early crocuses and smaller narcissi are swamped. But mowing men have an inborn dislike of taking the mower out of the shed after October.

I am not so tidy-minded about leaves. Except on the lawns, I like fallen leaves to be left, thinking of future leaf-mould, but Melanie grumbles about slugs and sneaks them away. However, she cannot easily sweep the lily-of-the-valley bed, nourished year after year by a fall of small cotoneaster leaves which rot down quickly, helped by a thin layer of manure.

Courageously climbing to the top rung of the ladder, Melanie has already pinned up and trained the climbing roses, I have deadheaded (not clipped) the lavender, and all over the garden we are getting into shape.

Dear Mother,

Well, I am in terrible shape. I abandoned the garden for several weeks in order to reconstruct the kitchen. Nick and I became so absorbed arranging the butcher's hooks that the garden was forgotten until I read your last letter. It is a bit of a sad sight. Apples, apples everywhere and every one a rotten one. The leaves are also thigh-high, so even looking for worms is a daunting task. To cap it all I have heavily clipped (not deadheaded) the lavender. If your garden is in the charge of an old-fashioned nanny, mine is in the hands of a wayward *au-pair*.

I had a vague go this weekend at tidying up the herbs, hewing down vast trunks of lovage and fennel and sweeping the leaves from the remaining parsley. Once I had begun clearing the leaves from the beds, it was rather pleasing to find odd things still flourishing underneath. Calypso's bed is doing well, the small violas are growing apace and her miniature rose is still flowering. I expect they'll die now I have exposed them to the winter frosts. Nick won't help at all with the leaf sweeping. He says he likes to wait until *all* the leaves have come off the trees so that you don't have to do it twice. The strong winds haven't helped. The edge of the thatch has just lifted enough to cover the garden with long strands of straw, which makes me nervous, as I prefer to have the roof over my head rather than below my feet. As if all this wasn't enough, the run between our two cottages is turning into the annual mud slide. So there we are, gloom, doom and despondency.

Did Vita ever feel this way?

Green Thoughts

Dear Clare,

Watching the leaves fluttering down from the whitebeams
(they are always the first to go), you said you wanted some
plants which keep their leaves in winter. Not churchyard
trees like ilex and yew, nor leathery shrubs like laurel and
skimmia, but plants with genuine bright green leaves to
cheer you up. 'Perhaps some herbaceous plants which don't
disappear completely, but keep some of their greenery.'

I can only say, like Christopher Wren, *circumspice*, for I
think you have quite a few winter foliage plants already. You
have that invaluable little sub-shrub, the perennial candytuft
or *Iberis sempervirens*, a positive cushion of bright green in
winter which will be joined by pure white flowers in spring.

You also have some of the herbaceous perennials which,
when they die down, retain a cluster of young leaves to mark
their position, as though to say don't dig us up by mistake,
we are here. The hardy geraniums do this to perfection –
look at your G. *endressii* and G. *macrorrhizum*, then at your
spotted pulmonarias, sedums, doronicum, creeping campanulas and London Pride. What you haven't got are violas.
Viola cornuta is a ravishing wild violet from the Pyrenees
from which many of our modern bedding pansies are bred.
The flowers are spurred and come in various mauves and in
white, and the leaves remain fresh-looking throughout the
year. My own dog violets also give me continuous pleasure,
seeding incontinently and making an impenetrable carpet of
dark green ground cover. I never sowed or planted them,
they just arrived, some purple and a few white.

Returning to the lighter greens, I will whisk past *Helleborus foetidus*, for you tell me I am obsessed with it, and here is
a more original thought. There is a wonderful iris called *I.
foetidissima* Variegata which rarely flowers but has tall,
dramatic evergreen leaves striped in green and cream. If it
would only rain seriously I could give you a token plant, but I

dare not split mine at present. I bought my first three plants after seeing a group of them at Esther Merton's one December day. She had planted them with hellebores (sorry) and the pretty little evergreen flowering currant called *Ribes laurifolium*, making an all-green group. I shamelessly copied the idea, but the ribes never flourished in my garden, though it still exists. I don't think it fancies my soil.

I know what you mean about leathery evergreen shrubs, I don't much like them either. They may make striking contrasts with deciduous shrubs, but their dark solidity doesn't warm the heart. Perhaps one or two variegated forms would be more cheerful. I really enjoy my variegated euonymus – *E. fortunei* Silver Queen and the coyly named Emerald 'n Gold – and my *Elaeagnus pungens* Maculata, its brilliant green and yellow leaves making a sunny splash on a grey day (reversing the usual order of events since the leaves go dingy in summer). Both shrubs, I must warn you, are very slow growing, for variegated plants have to make growth on a short allowance of chlorophyll, the green pigment which makes use of solar energy to turn carbon dioxide and water into food.

A swifter variegated evergreen, highly praised by Christopher Lloyd, is the buckthorn *Rhamnus alaterna* Argenteo-variegata, with green leaves edged with silver, but the other two are well worth waiting for.

Unrighteous Triumph

Dear Clare,

You win. There was a comical letter in *The Times* this morning from a gardener in Somerset noting that in early summer he bought three leggy tomato plants at a sale for 5p each. He planted them in the open and did nothing at all about them beyond an occasional watering – no feeding or nipping out of shoots – and gathered nearly 2,000 prime tomatoes, a triumph for a policy of *laissez-faire*. Outdoor tomato cultivation, according to the books, is a relentless campaign of seed-sowing under glass, planting out, hardening off, feeding, graduated watering, leaf removing, pinching out and inspection for a daunting variety of pests and diseases which may require spraying or dusting. All this was ignored by our friend from Somerset, meat for iconoclasts like you, a hollow laugh for nagging, guilt-ridden gardeners like me.

I look forward to follow-up letters in *The Times* from other idle but successful gardeners. Perhaps a man who grows fine camellias on chalk, a woman who dumps her tulip bulbs on the surface of the beds, possibly upside down, to enjoy a forest of flowers in May, a rose grower who never prunes, a man who scatters sweet peas in deep shade and picks bunches in the summer, another who grows celery on a hot, dry bank. I hope lots of readers write in, for there is a malicious pleasure in seeing the experts confounded.

Fine Shrubs

Dearest Clare,

From time to time I am stirred to write about a particular plant family, such as clematis or hellebores. My choice is not logical but personal, because one loves best the plants which have proved good friends in one's own peculiar conditions, and today I want to write about viburnums. The range is vast, most viburnums are splendid in shape, flower and leaf, and they grow with a will. It is high time to order shrubs now for planting in late autumn and winter, and it seems to me that you still have a bit of space.

My bank of *Viburnum plicatum* Mariesii is one of the most successful features of my garden. This marvellous shrub grows, as you know, in flat tiers of branches which really do justify the word 'architectural'. In early summer every branch is massed with white lacecap flowers, and however harsh the winter, they have never failed me. In autumn, the leaves turn crimson and there are scarlet berries, and even in winter the bare skeleton is worth looking at. A warning, however – you must give this plant twice the space you first thought of, for it can grow to fourteen feet across. Give it a huge hole and put plenty of compost, damp peat, leaf-mould, manure, or all four in the hole, for it is a shrub which in theory likes moisture, though it has flourished in my dry bank. Also, water it well in summer for the first two or three years.

There are several small viburnums which might suit your spaces better. *V. carlesii* Aurora makes a round shrub not more than four feet high, with ball-shaped flower clusters of rose pink changing to pale pink and then to white, with a delicious scent. There is a lovely hybrid bred from it called *V. juddii*, also scented, but a rather larger shrub.

V. tinus, or laurustinus, is one of the best of the winter-flowering shrubs and it is evergreen, with glossy leaves. Rumoured to be slightly tender, I did not try it for years, but I could kick myself, for my small plant did not flinch in the severe winter of 1987–88. I acquired it after noticing rather late in the day that the handsome laurustinus in the churchyard is strong and healthy in an exposed position. The flowers can be white or pinkish, and if you prefer pink, go for the variety called Eve Price.

One of the most beautiful viburnums is a British native, V. *opulus*, the guelder rose, with vine-shaped leaves, flat white scented flowers, and shiny red berries in autumn, the whole plant is gorgeous. But it likes lots of water, and in your garden or mine I would fear disappointment. It does grow in one garden in the village, but the site is flat and may hold water better than our sharply sloping ground – just another proof that a garden is never exactly the same as the one next door. It would be safer, if you want a large shrub which is not such a spreader as V. Mariesii, to grow V. *burkwoodii*, with white scented flowers which are larger than those of my dear V. *carlesii*, and very dramatic indeed when the shrub has grown to its full height. It would make a fine specimen in your front lawn where you could admire it through the window of your smart new kitchen.

The viburnums, which belong surprisingly to the same family as honeysuckles, the *Caprifoliaceae*, are an enormous tribe filling many pages of *Bean's Trees and Shrubs*, and it is a treat to see a collection in a botanic garden. Most of them are both spectacular and easy to grow, virtues which do not always go hand in hand. Gardeners who travel about as much as you do soon learn to bless hardy, accommodating shrubs which take care of themselves. It is cheering to come back from a trip to find the herbaceous plants flagging and the annuals gone to seed, but the shrubs in great fettle, not having missed you at all.

November

A Woman's Work

Dear Clare,

Watching you battle with the brush-cutter, the grass having put on a late spurt with all the vigour of spring, I felt that Women's Lib. is no longer a distant prospect, but a battle won.

Yet it may prove a Pyrrhic victory. If women could have equality in education, jobs, finance and political power I would swing along with it, but now they seem to require large biceps, too. When I see a man sitting in a deckchair on the lawn while his wife chops the logs, I feel that women have made a bad bargain. They are no better off than the Greek peasant woman whose husband rides the donkey while she trudges behind loaded with a stack of brushwood.

I have been pondering the division of labour in the garden where women increasingly take on the heavy duties. I was looking at an old gardening manual giving week-by-week instructions on jobs to be done, and there was scarcely one which I have attempted at any time in my gardening life. But I took a snap poll among three women gardeners of your generation asking if they would tackle such jobs and the foolish creatures said yes to ninety per cent of them. I will quote a few.

Protect fruit trees growing on walls and flowering climbers of doubtful hardiness by lightly thatching them with spruce boughs. (All three said they would do this.)

Lawns to be raked, spiked and top-dressed. (Could manage, but too boring.)

Complete tar-oil spraying of cherries, plums etc. (All said could manage, but one did not fancy the awful protective clothing.)

Trench for celery. (All said they were doing it all the time, never stopped trenching.)

Give a final mowing to lawns and run over grassy banks with a hover machine. (As above, heavy, noisy machines welcomed.)

Waterlogged land may require drainage. (All refused this, I am glad to say.)

Complete training of climbers on walls and tie in any straggling branches of climbers growing up trees. (A slight reluctance here. Only one said she would do both walls and trees, one said she drew the line at trees as they were probably rotten anyway, one said she felt giddy if the trees swayed.)

We have certainly come a long way from the ancient tradition whereby the man of the house managed the trees, hedges, shrubs, vegetables, path-laying, cartage and other heavy physical work, while the wife grew the flowers and herbs and kept the chickens. I myself would prefer it this way and have no false pride about calling in a man to cut my 12-foot hedges, and, as you know, I am terrified of machinery. But you, dear skinny daughter, heaving and hacking as you do, seem to have developed an invisible muscular strength which I never aspired to. Do you ever regret it?

Dear Mother,

Yes. I have over the years drawn the line at car maintenance, not because of the physical hardship, but because it is still the one task that the opposite sex seems happy to indulge in.

When it comes to gardening I will hew and hack with the best of them. I do this because I foolishly think that if I am spotted dragging wheelbarrows or scything grass, I will be rescued. I still believe that from the security of his armchair, Nick may feel a twinge of guilt and wrest the tools from my grasp. This does not happen very often. Usually he will amble forth and say, 'Your toes will be severed if the machine falls backwards, put on your wellingtons,' and then go back inside.

Perhaps I am being unfair. Nick has been pretty good this year, but he does insist on the loads being shared; in fact, he maintains I am stronger than he is. As you point out, I have no muscles, but I have a great deal of willpower which can and does move not only mountains but banks, roots, manure etc. I do enjoy splitting logs. This requires no real strength at all, just accurate blows, and is splendid therapy for dispelling aggression.

I would frankly rather not do any of it. It produces very little satisfaction, apart from getting a job done without having to wait around. All my female friends feel the same, masculine energy is on the decline while more and more manual tasks fall our way. I have the added disadvantage of inheriting your height. It is hopeless trying to look weak, pathetic and six foot.

What is the answer? I shall croon to Calypso while she sleeps, 'Marry a Rothschild, marry a Rothschild', on the offchance she will opt for a life without drudgery, and possibly send out the under-gardener to help her poor enfeebled mother. By that time I will probably be carrying not only the brushwood, but Nick and the donkey, too.

Suttons Seeds

Dear Clare,

The now hideous town of Reading was once to me the Promised Land. It was here that my isolated but adored country holidays began, here that my brother and I were met at the station in early childhood by a farmer and his wife in a trap, and later by the village taxi. The approach to Reading in the train was made glorious not only by excitement but by the brilliant floral display blazing from the trial ground of Suttons Seeds. Here was a multi-coloured mosaic, covering several acres, of plants in all the flashy colours which children love.

Although Suttons disloyally moved years ago to Torquay, theirs is still my favourite seed catalogue, and it arrived last week. The Dobies and Thompson & Morgan catalogues also yield treasures, but I am faithful to Suttons, with its parade of gaudy flowers and prime vegetables and its practical tips, and from habit I will order far more seeds than I can possibly sow.

Most will be hardy annuals (half-hardy bedding plants I'll buy at a garden centre), and I want flowers which are good for cutting, and flowers which bloom late, helping to fill the August gaps. All will be sown *in situ* in the spring, and all are in Suttons' list.

Salvia sclarea, or clary, is a favourite, and for once I get a mixed packet. The flowers (composed of bracts, not petals, but what does it matter?) come in soft purple, pink and white, and flower late. So does the tall annual mallow, *Lavatera trimestris*, a rather coarse plant which looks best, I think, in the white Mont Blanc variety. Shirley poppies and Blue Diadem cornflowers – I detest the pink ones – do not flower for long but are irresistible, as are a few giant sunflowers to gratify one's lingering childhood tastes, and I will order an extra packet for Calypso. Sweet peas, of course, in colours which I vary from year to year, but I always include Cream Beauty and the wine-red Beaujolais, plus a packet of the small-flowered but richly scented grandiflora varieties. Oh yes, and I need some nasturtiums to cover some of my scruffier banks.

I want to try two annuals this year which I have not grown before. One is the corn marigold which is now rare as a wild plant, though I saw it in September on my Scotland holiday, in a cornfield near Inverness. I used to find it in Berkshire cornfields years ago, but even then it was uncommon, and I was delighted to see it, with other wild flowers, in Suttons' list. And for my garden sink, I might try *Dimorphotheca aurantiaca*, a daisy which flowers over a long period, but it has shiny petals, and I may not like it. I do not need to order Love-in-a-mist and *Limnanthes douglasii*, for they have sown themselves.

Though hardy annuals are easy to grow, they are not 'trouble-free', to use an optimistic gardening catchphrase. They all need sun, and it is difficult to find places for them where they will not be swamped in infancy by herbaceous plants. One must clear a definite patch of ground for each variety and mark it clearly with a label. And since they will not have time to grow deep roots, they must be watered. A dry summer is hard on them, and sometimes they flag in August but put on a good show in September. And they must be religiously deadheaded, for if they set seed they will cease to flower.

Also on my Suttons' order form will go parsley, radish, rocket and cos lettuce, the last three just for fun, a reminder of my once well-filled vegetable garden.

Scarlet or Gold?

Dear C,

At the RHS they are known as 'the rhododendron men', the great gardeners who are revelling now in their broad acid acres ablaze with autumn colour. They walk among the fires set alight by trees and shrubs from north America and Japan, among them liquidambar, fothergilla, Japanese acers and amelanchier. But you and I live modestly among quieter colours, for the autumn foliage of most chalk-loving trees and shrubs is gentler, and above eye-level my garden is a haze of leaves which are golden or tawny.

My favourite of all trees in autumn is the British native field maple, *Acer campestre*, of which I have just one in the boundary hedge and which must be very old. I wish I had planted more of them long ago, for their golden autumn leaves are exceptionally beautiful. The chestnut, the old twisted oak and the *Prunus subhirtella* have also turned bronze or gold, as did the sorbuses, but their leaves have gone already. Many of the shrubs are gold, too, especially the rugosa roses and the *Spiraea arguta*, which I thought two years ago was dying of coral spot, but on the local forester's advice I cut it to the ground, and it has made a healthy new bush. I imagine that your own rugosas and spiraea are colouring, too – the best of the rugosas in this respect is Frau Dagmar Hastrup – which also carries enormous hips.

There is a little red to be seen here at a lower level, with some of the viburnums, geraniums and the kolkwitzia turning crimson, and the leaves of *Euphorbia polychroma* a rosy pink, but the hostas and lilies-of-the valley turn gold before they disappear underground.

The luckiest thing about gardening is that real gardeners like what they have got. The rhododendron men would perhaps despise my undramatic autumn trees, and though I love to visit their brilliant woods, I do not want them for myself. Even if I could plant my garden with fiery maples in the image of New England in the fall, I would not do it, and though I think a parrotia is one of the few crimson trees which would grow well here I would not plant it. My yellow and gold and russet seem to me best in our particular kind of English landscape, with its gentle greens, brown ploughland and watercolour sky. It is not by chance that so many of the best English painters have been artists in watercolour.

Staying On

Dear Clare,

I have been firmly spoken to about overdoing the autumn clear-up by Esther Merton, no less. Esther is the queen bee of herbaceous gardening – every time I turn on the TV I see either a single parent who is not getting enough benefit, or else Esther discussing the *compositae* with some other pundit. She told me I should not cut down my borders in the autumn.

All Esther's borders are invisibly propped through the summer by wigwams of pea-sticks, and she leaves these in place through the winter, too, with the plants inside. The flower stalks wither, of course, but the pea-sticks keep them under control in their decay, as in their prime. 'I like it brown but tidy', Esther says, looking down the twin borders which are fully clothed, as in July, but in the sombre colours of shrivelled flowers.

The main purpose of this preservation is, of course, frost protection, and Esther has pulled many plants through a hard winter which have died in gardens round about. The flower stems provide a 3- or 4-foot frost barrier and the clumps of old basal leaves protect the young leaves when they appear, which may be too early in a mild spell for their own good. Even really tender things, like the shrubby salvias, have a good chance of surviving to make larger plants next summer, though one plant is always taken up and transferred to the greenhouse for future cuttings. But Esther likes the winter borders aesthetically, too. She prefers the tiers of vertical stalks to flat earth, and admires the patterns of hoar-frost which make the achilleas and sedums and Michaelmas daisies sparkle. She admits that there is a family sigh of relief when the big chop-down is carried out at last in the spring.

I don't think I could myself forego the pleasure of the October clear-up, but I will try to be more selective as to which plants are trimmed and which are left.

Odd Corners

Dear C,

I have seen quite a few large gardens this year, where vistas, sweeps, and group plantings are of the essence, but most people have small gardens which they work themselves, and one good way of planning them is to make 'corners'. This suits busy people like you, as you can happily tackle a corner in the odd half-hour between turning up Calypso's new trousers and putting on the soup, while a big expanse of garden might daunt you. A 'corner' is not necessarily angular, and may be just a part of the garden, perhaps a flowerbed or a group of trees, which is self-contained.

I never knew a better garden for corners than John Piper's. Some of the corners are exactly that in a geometric sense, as the main garden is a large walled rectangle with an extra old brick wall running across the middle, but there are lots of other rounded corners, such as a huge old apple tree with underplanting beyond the kitchen and a terrace for pots outside the greenhouse, including pots of morning glory. All are planted in a cottagey manner.

One corner in the main garden has an apple tree with a white rambler growing up it and snowdrops in the ground. It could be weeded and cultivated within half an hour. Another has a pear tree with lilies-of-the-valley, hellebores, rosemary and thyme. Another has a damson with Paul's Lemon Pillar (one of Osbert's favourite roses, it is the one with large white flowers near my back door), honeysuckle and two euphorbias – E. *polychroma* and E. *griffithii* Fireglow with flame-coloured bracts – and also *Helleborus viridis*, the small species which grows wild in chalky woods. Another corner has a magnolia surrounded by John's 'thistle nursery' – he is a great man for thistles, both in his paintings and his garden, and has a lot of *Echinops ritro*, the globe thistle, and *Onopordum acanthium*, the Scotch thistle, both of which burst into flower in August, the month which is so deadly at my cottage.

Even his otherwise strictly disciplined vegetable garden
has clumps at the corners of all the flowers one likes best,
auriculas, herbs, the winter-flowering *Iris unguicularis* and
crown imperials.

I myself have quite a lot of corners, mostly imposed by the
eccentric site and by the large single trees, including my
walnut (which I grew from a nut and must now be some forty
years old) and my chestnut beside the tumbledown shed
which is flatteringly called the garage. I have dealt with some
of these corners well, others are wasted. I have found plenty
of plants which will grow in the shade of the walnut, such as
Mahonia aquifolium, snowdrops and *Iris foetidissima.* But the
chestnut needs many more spring bulbs beneath it, and I
want to plant aconites and the pale blue scilla, *S. tuberge-
niana,* which flowers very early, to precede the daffodils
which are, I fear, a dull variety.

Your garden may not cry out for corners, for you have your
own peculiar system of small beds, each with a fruit tree and
a bit of underplanting. But I do feel that more could be made
of your copse, with more interesting small trees and more
plants beneath. The trees could be quite sparsely planted to
give that desirable amenity, dappled light.

Dear Mother,

You have referred a couple of times during the year to my
'quirky' gardening techniques, and now in your last letter to
my 'peculiar small beds'. I am beginning to feel that I am
sitting in the front row of an Edna Everage evening having
all my little nooks and crannies probed. I shy away from the
designer layouts I sometimes see in gardening articles,
perhaps this is a mistake, but they seem to be geared to
rectangular areas, and are not suited to my hummocks.

You were very courageous with your initial garden design,
including a major earthwork in the construction of the
sunken garden. Where did you put the earth? When I made

my 'eccentric' dining-area, I ended up with so much spare soil that I had the makings of a rockery.

The logic behind my 'peculiar small beds' is that I can keep altering the shape to suit. As plants grow larger, I just heave out a few more clods of turf. If I fancy a new shrub round the back, no problem, I dig a suitable hole and in it goes. This cunning method ensures that the size of each bed is contained until you need more. One day all the small beds are going to join up and I will have a ravishing vista stretching across the garden.

I do think it unfair that John Piper's corners mould aesthetically into his garden, while mine merely look marooned, but there it is. Meantime, I would like no more references, however lovingly meant, to my gardening quirks. I am still sensitive from the 'grill-a-parent' interview at Calypso's school five years ago when the headmistress, ushering me out, whispered, 'Well, we always like the token eccentric here, Mrs Hastings.'

Tulipomania

Dearest Clare,

Heaven forgive me if I have hurt your feelings with my careless talk. For 'eccentric' read 'original' throughout. I adore your garden, which could only be yours, and am bored stiff by gardens out of a pattern book. I have had far more pleasure in your ever-hospitable garden this summer than in any other. As a peace offering, I have bought you some striped tulips, for I know you share my tulipomania, a passion for tulips which brought the staid Dutch nation to the verge of bankruptcy in the seventeenth century. A century later a similarly obsessed Turkish sheik wrote a lyrical book about tulips describing the pearl of his collection as having 'the colour of the violet and the curved form of the new moon'.

Without going quite so barmy, I do find tulips irresistible in all their guises – small charming species, large satiny Darwins, striped or frilled tulips, tulips with pointed petals and slender waists, tulips with patterned leaves. Most are so easy to grow that you put a bulb in and a flower comes up – all they ask is sunshine and good drainage. Plant them now, though December is not too late.

In up-and-down gardens like yours and mine, regiments of tulips are unsuitable, though they have a military splendour in the parks. The tall ones look best in groups of one colour (not jumbled up) in a mixed border. The small-flowered species and their hybrids can find a home in odd corners, or they can be planted as a ribbon of colour in a narrow bed or under a wall. Many tulips will last for years, so there is no need to lift them after flowering. The only tulips I replant every year are the dark purple ones, as the flowers get smaller in their second season.

You can choose your tulips from a catalogue, but the postage comes dear, so I suggest you get them from a garden shop. My special favourites are, of the early species, almost any with bi-coloured flowers like the red-and-white *T. clusiana* which I am offering you now. Of the tall May-flowering tulips, the nearly black Queen of the Night. Of the lily-flowered tulips with pointed petals, the claret-red Captain Fryatt grouped near the pure white White Triumphator. And I wax as lyrical as the Turkish sheik about the frilled parrot tulips, but they must be planted in a sheltered spot, for their heads are so large and heavy that a high wind may snap them off.

Tulips also look splendid in pots and tubs, or grouped among shrubs so long as they get enough sun. A friend of mine with a wild garden likes to plant an unusual tulip here and there to surprise you, perhaps a rare Rembrandt variety springing out of a background of ivy. Wherever you plant them, they never disappoint.

December

The Garden Wakes

Dear Clare,

The gloom and doom of the dying year, inescapable in a city, dispel as soon as I enter my garden. In December, it is reborn. December the First is my New Year's Day, and far from lying in a deathlike sleep, the garden is bursting with energy. Shoots of this, flowers of that, plenty of colour. You and Calypso are looking forward to January, when you take up your stylish yachting life, and join Rodney's party sailing from island to island in some tropical sea. (The only real yacht I ever joined was by mistake, when some young friends and I were marooned on a sandbank off Bosham, and were rescued and given lunch by Gordon Selfridge on what looked like a Cunard liner.) But before you take wing, a long dark December lies ahead of you, and some cheerful winter plants would enliven the sombre scene.

Green and yellow are the colours of the month at my cottage. The island beds are inland seas of self-sown *Helleborus foetidus*, the apple-green buds already rearing above the dark green leaves. My best winter shrub is a foliage shrub, totally frost-proof, *Elaeagnus pungens* Maculata, which I suggested to you a few weeks ago. The winter jasmine is out and the *Mahonia japonica* is in tight bud, full of promise. The winter-sweet buds ought to be forming, but this lovely scented shrub has always been a disappointment here.

Many other plants are on the move, such as the whitebeam, *Sorbus aria* Lutescens, with swelling buds impervious to bad weather. The *Prunus subhirtella* Autumnalis is fit for picking. The *Euonymus fortunei* Silver Queen looks particularly fresh in winter when its variegated leaves have a tinge of pink. So when the first red-flowered hellebore, *H. atrorubens*, bursts into flower punctually on Boxing Day, and when the first bulbs pop up in January, they will not be the pioneers. Earlier plants have been proving that the gardener's year starts in December.

A Time for Formality

Dear Clare,

As you know, I am both by nature and experience a cottage gardener. I like the plants. I like the romanticism. I like the social mix whereby grand plants and garden features rub shoulders with humble ones, lilies with daisies, a classic statue in one corner, a rustic arch in another. I like the mutations of a cottage garden, colours and phases of growth changing from week to week. A formal garden is a more constant thing, almost indifferent to the seasons, and one must admit that it can look serenely impressive at this mushy time of year.

No, I am not doing a *volte-face*, or denying the small signs that my deciduous garden, so recently put to bed, is already waking up. But I have been visiting a garden in Wiltshire with winter beauty of a different kind. It is planned in a formal Italian manner, changes but little over the year, and looks splendid now. On a terrace by the house there are rows of large pots of hydrangeas, their huge clusters of flowers faded to chestnut brown, but in mint condition. On another terrace there are tubs with clipped bay trees. There are masses of evergreens – a grove of ilex, obelisks of yew, box hedges clipped tight. There are stone steps, paths and statues. Nearly all the flowers in the garden are bedding plants; the summer ones were taken out long ago and replaced with tidy wallflowers for the spring. Nothing looks sodden or down-at-heel.

Most of the formal gardens I have seen in England are very grand, like Renishaw, home of the Sitwell family, or Garsington Manor near Oxford, where Lady Ottoline Morrell's house-parties in the nineteen-twenties reeked of Bloomsbury, and the Bells and Woolfs and Stracheys wove their complicated sexual patterns when they were not writing their challenging books. (Their energy was stupendous.) But formal gardening, which went out of fashion for a long time under the influence of William Robinson, has found a place in quite small gardens over the last decade, and pot gardens, knot gardens, chequerboard herb gardens, topiary, trained fruit trees and standard roses can be found fitted into mixed gardens of half an acre or less. In midwinter, when there is no competition from daffodils or roses, formality makes its strongest statement.

I cannot imagine you tying in the shoots of a row of espalier pear trees, or see myself clipping Elizabethan scrollwork of box and santolina, but I do genuinely admire formal gardening. I fear I have weighted my letters too much on the cottagey side, and am, in short, determined to be broadminded.

Bad Gardens

Dear Clare,

I have written much this year about the beautiful and the good. Enthusiastic gardening writers are apt to get carried away by the many lovely things they see and it is easy for the reader to get the impression that all English gardens are beautiful, luxuriant, fragrant, mysterious, rich in surprises, painted with an artist's palette, miracles of harmonious planting, and so on and so forth. The eye is carried admiringly upwards, downwards, sideways etc until one is almost squinting with delight. But there are bad gardens, too, which mercifully one soon forgets, like the pains of childbirth, but perhaps as the year ends one should be a little more critical and ask an unusual question. What makes a bad garden?

One common cause of bad gardening afflicts the keen gardener, not the lazy one. He (or she) has fallen under too many influences. He reads a lot, sees a lot, and takes advice from everybody, so that his garden is full of conflicting ideas. A sensitive gardener with catholic tastes may grow many things from lime-loving alpines to peat-loving pieris, but he will keep them apart, providing a different background for each. But I know gardens where you can see, all in one eyeful, specimen Japanese maples in the lawn, a cottage border with hollyhocks and pansies to one side, and a knot garden somewhere in the middle. The result is not the expression of one gardener's taste, but a mess of pottage. Often the gardener himself is not happy with the result and makes bad worse by consulting more and more people, who each give different advice.

Bad gardens of another sort are created by an unbridled use of colour, and summer bedding plants are the chief culprits. The clash of the harsh colours of marigolds, busy lizzies, *Salvia splendens* and begonias gives a shock rather than a happy glow. The gardener is often technically skilled and raises perfect plants in the greenhouse, but he gives no thought to their arrangement. You may well say that no garden is a bad garden if the gardener likes it, and you are right. But it is gardening at a low level. No outsider having seen the garden once would want to look at it twice, for it can be comprehended at a glance, and there is nothing to see in winter.

Another class of bad garden is the product of too much money. It is packed with showy and expensive garden furnishings which dominate the plants. White seats and white pyramids for supporting roses give the look of a hotel ballroom, and even worse are those costly swings upholstered in cretonne patterned with tropical flowers which are larger and brighter than anything which grows. Miss Jekyll thought that garden furniture should be an inconspicuous comfort, and that seats should be in dark colours, preferably brown, and I cannot forgive the restorers of Monet's famous garden at Giverny for painting the seats and bridge in the brightest green in the paint manufacturer's showcard. A swimming-pool can also be an eyesore. If a gardener wants an athlete's pool with diving boards, changing rooms and a shower, why doesn't he hide it away in a hedged enclosure?

Run-of-the-mill gardeners like you and me will have bad patches in our gardens, perhaps ill-planned steps or paths or planting mistakes, but I hope there is none of the real ugliness which arises from pretentiousness or from lifting ideas indiscriminately instead of making a personal choice.

Year's End

Darling Clare,

We're at the end of the year, and I have written to you about our gardening lives every week, even when on holiday. I hope I haven't sounded too pontifical.

Your garden remains very much your own thing, with your own design and specialities, such as fine sweet peas and a barbecue corner scented with honeysuckle. But I think I have helped with plant suggestions (I see many new plants springing up in adventurous corners), and by passing on my enthusiasm for the soil itself, which I strive to make crumbly, wormy and well-fed.

You have assured me from time to time that you have enjoyed getting my letters – and have responded with some pretty crisp replies. I certainly enjoyed writing them, and in the process have cleared my own mind about many gardening problems and controversies. Perhaps one always writes partly for oneself. Autobiographers write to excuse their bad behaviour, novelists write to expose their wrongs, especially ex-wives seeking revenge on former husbands, didactic authors write to learn about their subjects – Ruskin admitted this was a stimulus.

Another bonus for me is that I have roused myself from indolence and resolved to take a lot of my own advice. I have ordered new plants, I have taken steps about compost, I am looking for fresh places for new roses, and I have condemned some inferior shrubs. I hope to write to you at the end of next year reporting some marvellous progress.

Best love from your mother.

Index